Accounting with Sage

Accounting with Sage

David Royall

Pitman

PITMAN PUBLISHING
128 Long Acre, London WC2E 9AN

A Division of Longman Group UK Limited

© Longman Group UK Limited 1992

First published in Great Britain 1992

British Library Cataloguing-in-Publication Data
A catalogue record for this book is available
from the British Library

ISBN 0–273–03811–7

Printed and bound in Great Britain

In loving memory of my brother, Richard.

Contents

Preface

The main aim of this book is to give students and practitioners a sound knowledge of the Sage Sterling range of business software in Accountancy and to develop skills in bookkeeping and financial analysis.

The range of software includes in-depth coverage of the following packages:

Bookkeeper
Accountant
Accountant Plus
Financial Controller

This book is carefully organised so that readers who are using any of the above versions of Sage can benefit from its material. This is because **Accountant Plus** is a sub-set of **Financial Controller**, and in turn **Accountant** is a sub-set of **Accountant Plus**; at the bottom of the range, **Bookkeeper** is a sub-set of **Accountant**.

The range also has networked versions which will be examined where appropriate.

Any business person, particularly in a small firm with little money for this kind of development, will find this book extremely useful and will find they can probably implement Sage Accounts as they work through the book without the use of expensive consultancy services or training courses.

Included in this book are three case studies showing how actual companies went about computerising their accounting functions using the Sage package. The case studies are varied, in order to demonstrate a wide degree of experience and approach to implementation.

Although some previously-gained computing skills would be an advantage in learning computerised accounts, it is by no means essential. This book assumes no previous computing knowledge. When embarking on computerised accounts, you will soon appreciate that bookkeeping and accounting skills are more important than computing ones. Consequently, this book seeks to cover as much bookkeeping and accounting as it does computing. It is very much a 'teach yourself' guide.

Accounting with Sage offers practical guidance to Sage users by giving an opportunity to reflect on the use and application of the packages away from the computer as well as structured guidance on the package while using the computer. In other words, the book offers advice and guidance about *how you* can achieve tasks rather than just how tasks are done. A good example of this is when certain activities should be 'batch processed' rather than simply carried out as tasks on an *ad hoc* basis.

This book has a semi-tutorial approach and can best be used by reading it in the chapter sequence presented and with access to a Sage package. At certain points in the book, you will be prompted to skip sections if they do not relate to your version of the Sage package.

The first chapter gives an introduction to the concepts of computing, and the basic requirements to computerise accounts and methods which a business ought to adopt. It also explains how to install the package on your computer. You will then work through the Sage modules in a way that develops your skill and understanding, both of the package and the basic functions that the modules attempt to computerise. You will be encouraged to understand exactly what the computer is trying to do, rather than simply operating the system in a mechanical way.

The book will be of particular help to those students of accounting who are working for a qualification with one of the accounting professional boards such as the AAT, ACCA or ICMA. It not only deals with fundamental bookkeeping and accounting principles, but also deals with computing and data processing concepts in an integrated manner, a requirement of almost all the professional accounting qualifications.

It will also serve as a useful text for students and tutors involved with BTEC National and Higher qualifications in Business and Finance, PEI Computerised Accounts Levels 1 and 2 and those students studying Small Business Systems and Concepts on BTEC courses in Business and Computing areas. With the growing emphasis on the need to integrate many business and information technology skills in a practical way, this text and the appropriate computing resources offer a method of meeting such requirements.

By the time you have worked through this book, you should have gained an insight into the way a business information system operates, as well as gaining invaluable skills in computerised accounts.

DR

1 Introduction

Using a computer to manage a set of accounts and stock system for a business is not in itself a panacea to all those problems typically encountered when running a business. One of the first points to consider is whether the business can significantly benefit from using a computer and, if it can, what is the best way of going about it. In considering the purchase of a computer system and associated software, there are a number of procedures to go through.

1 IDENTIFYING THE NEED TO USE A COMPUTER

One of the starting points for a business is to decide whether or not a computer would be of benefit. This can be a difficult need to assess if you are not aware of what a computer can and cannot do.

It is always wise for someone to investigate how a computer could perform tasks and gain a little experience by attending exhibitions, short courses at the local college of further education, or even contact a business associate who uses a computer in order to benefit from their experience. For most businesses a computer, if properly used and administered, can be of great benefit to the accounting and financial management function.

An important first requirement is to assess exactly what work the business wants the computer to do. Also, by establishing the amount of work that has to be done, you will help the supplier to ensure that an adequate system is provided for your needs. When a business decides to purchase a motor vehicle, it must have some idea of the amount of work such a vehicle has to do and the amount of freight it has to carry in order to purchase a vehicle that is capable of handling the work. Exactly the same must apply to a computer system.

Having established these requirements, it is a good idea to put such details in writing and send them to a number of potential suppliers to see what they can offer. Such a document may include the following:

- The nature of your business

- What a computer would be expected to do

- The amount of information processing expected from a system

- The number of staff currently doing the work and approximately how much time is spent now on such processing activities

There is no reason, of course, why a more experienced person cannot purchase a complete system through a magazine, catalogue or high street shop and make a success of using it.

However 'ideal' a resulting system might be, its success will depend upon the way it is installed and maintained.

The essence of a computerised accounting system is no different to that of a manual system. The introduction of calculators has not altered the basic rules of arithmetic and mathematics and, likewise, the introduction of computers has not altered the basic rules of bookkeeping and accounts – just our approach.

One of the most difficult aspects of using a computerised system will be the process of setting it up. In most businesses, transactions are being generated on a very regular basis and details about such things as stock quantities, customer accounts, and so on would be difficult to assess accurately at any given point of time. When setting up a computer system, we will need to enter all the details about the state of a company's accounts before we can start. The problem is that by the time all the required information has been compiled and entered to the system, it has become out of date. The problem is the classic one of trying to alter a moving target.

Many of the above issues will be raised in this book, with the first activity of installing the Sage package on to your computer being dealt with in this chapter. Also this book gives ideas about how to overcome some of the problems and dilemmas facing a firm which wishes to computerise an accounting system and then operate it.

2 SOME EXPECTED BENEFITS OF USING COMPUTERS

Time-saving in transactions processing and the production of a series of reports are obvious benefits we would expect from computerising accounts. The basic principle of any accounting system is depicted in Fig 1.1.

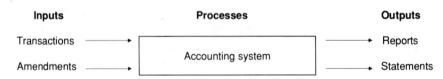

Fig. 1.1

The aim of a computerised accounting system is to perform the processing stage electronically; which should be performed much more quickly than if it were done manually. However, transactions and amendment details have to get into the process in the correct form, in the correct order and in a timely manner. Although there is scope to use electronic methods of entering some of this data, it will require a good deal of human input and initiative, and an organised way of doing things. Further time-saving can be achieved by automatic output of reports such as details about whether the firm is making a profit or loss, customer statements, sales analysis, cash and bank statements. Such reports and statements can be produced by the computer searching through information already generated and saved by the accounting system.

Effective reporting improves the decision-making process. For example, a computer system should be capable of detecting when a customer appears to be running up excessive debts with the company, offering the chance to take action before these get out of hand. Another area is the need to remain within budgets. Many business expenses can become too great if they are not checked at regular intervals. What a computerised accounts system should be capable of is an activity called **exception reporting**; a process of issuing early-warning messages to operators when something appears to be out of order. In a manual system, the situation often occurs that errors or unwanted transactions go unnoticed until too late or until they have already incurred unnecessary costs to the firm.

For many businesses, the need to produce monthly and annual returns such as VAT and payroll can be time-consuming, tedious and unrewarding. The use of a computer system can be an effective tool to speed up the process and reduce the work of producing lengthy reports with large amounts of figure-work. In many cases, firms find that they can use computer printouts or even data on computer disks instead of having to complete official forms.

Improved accuracy may be another of the more obvious benefits of any kind of computer system, which is especially the case with accounting, where numerous calculations have to be carried out.

More job satisfaction and more effective use of operator time can be an added bonus with computerisation. For example, if a firm computerises its stock records, an operator's job of maintaining records will be much the same as in a manual system. However, with instant reporting facilities available, such as a list of all stock items that may be in short supply, the operator can extract and produce details much faster. This will allow the operator to keep a much closer check on stock levels. Also, if time can be saved in producing stock reports, the operator may have more time to 'chase up' suppliers who are not delivering on time or 'shop around' the market for better suppliers and products.

Many more benefits of computerisation will become apparent as you work your way through this book. It is worth noting that the extent of the benefits will vary from business to business, with each one deriving different benefits. It may even be the case that a business can derive no benefit at all from computerisation because there is insufficient data processing to justify the cost and effort.

Once a computer system is working properly, managers will often find themselves extracting reports that could not be achieved under a manual system within a timescale that would serve a useful purpose. The improved reporting and analysis that can be achieved by computerisation should improve the whole decision-making process within an organisation.

3 DIFFERING COMPUTER SYSTEMS

In choosing a computer system you will need to consider both the hardware and software. In most instances, a decision about the software will be made first. Software instructs the computer system about the processing of data. Such software will come at two levels.

The first level is the computer's **operating system**. This software, as its name suggests, will operate all parts of the computer system, including keyboard input, screen output, printing, and the internal processing and storage of data inside the computer itself. All computer systems have an operating system, but not necessarily the same operating system. Operating systems include Microsoft Disk Operating System (MS-DOS), Operating System/2 (OS/2) UNIX and Novell. Such operating systems are designed for different computer systems and are constantly changing in nature. As computers become more advanced and their operating environment has altered, the operating system must also change.

The second level of software is the **applications package**. This adds to the software by offering the added features required to perform specific tasks, such as accounting. When purchasing an applications package, such as Sage, it is important that the correct version is purchased to match the operating system. In turn, the operating system must be a correct match with the computer system. In others words, **compatibility** must exist between operating system and applications package.

Deciding on the hardware needed will become easier once the software decision has been made and it is clear about the amount of work required of the system. The type of system that would normally meet the needs of a small to medium-sized business would fall into one of three categories: stand-alone, network or a multi-user/tasking system.

Stand alone

Such a system will consist of one screen, one keyboard, one disk drive and enough memory to run the software. For a firm with relatively small data processing needs and no requirement for more than one operator to be at a keyboard at any time, such a system could prove quite adequate. In the event of a business purchasing such a system, it would probably be advisable to have a system with a **hard disk**, where the operating system is already loaded.

A network of micros

This allows the linking up of microcomputers together in such a way that they are able to share information and enable the centralisation of the data processing system. In other words, someone working on a computer on a network system can update information on a customer and any other person on another machine which is also on the network is aware of the update if they inspect that customer's account. Such a linked set-up is of particular use in larger organisations that require the accounting and related data processing function to be divided between a number of staff. It also allows management the facility of extracting reports without having to disturb the accounts staff.

Such networks are not fixed in size. They can vary according to the requirements of the organisation, from two microcomputers on a network to dozens of microcomputers. Firms should always take advice when deciding on the number of microcomputers to network together. Too many on a network may lead to congestion.

Multi-user/tasking

Such a set-up is similar to that of a network. The difference lies in the fact that the system is one computer with a number of **terminals** attached to it. In other words, each keyboard is not a computer in its own right. Such a system means that an operating system such as Novell will be used.

Choosing which type of system is appropriate for which kind of business is not an easy task. It is important to bear in mind that any software package will not work on every machine. Compatibility across a system is a key issue in the decision-making process.

4 PRINTING

All users of computerised accounts will need to print information such as customer statements, invoices, order forms, audit trails, or reports. It is worth noting that it is unlikely computerising the accounting functions will significantly reduce the amount of paper used. In fact many new users have found that the computer results in more paper, not less.

Different types of printers are available for computer systems. Any firm using computers will need to assess how many printers are required and the kind of quality of printing that needs to be achieved.

The most commonly-used printer is the **dot matrix printer**. This produces character images on to paper by dot patterns, one character at a time. Most matrix printers are capable of printing a full page (A4 size) of text in under a minute and at a very reasonable quality. For most accounting functions' printing output, this kind of printer is both economic and adequate. Stationery for such printers includes continuous paper (fanfold), which is a cheap way of acquiring printed output.

For improved output quality, a **laser printer** is another option. The quality of print is better, the machines are not as noisy and they accept standard-sized single sheets of paper. For most accounts reports, this is probably a little extravagant. For graphics output and good quality letter production, a laser printer may be a viable option.

Other types of printers are available for serving differing types of needs. The term **hard copy** is often used to refer to printed output, as opposed to **soft copy**, which refers to screen output.

5 STAFF TRAINING

Another major issue in implementing computerised accounts will be the need to ensure that staff are adequately prepared and trained, which can be done in a number of ways:

a Purchase a system and the required software from a company which also offers staff training.
b Send a member of staff on a course. Such courses are available at differing times of the year from both private institutions and local colleges of further education.
c Employ someone who is already trained.
d Hope that an employee can learn the package and computer system as they implement it, giving them time to research and experiment. (Although this option is extremely risky, it is often used).

Staff training is an expense often overlooked. Poorly trained staff can lead to the downfall of any system, computerised or not.

In conclusion, anyone responsible for computerisation should be aware that a certain amount of time and patience is required. Computerising a manual bookkeeping system cannot be done overnight; it may well take weeks or months. In Chapter 10 there are three case studies which will put this into some kind of perspective and offer a much more detailed analysis for implementing computerised accounts.

THE DATA PROTECTION ACT 1984

Most firms that make extensive use of computers for accounts, payroll and any other applications that involve details of personal individuals would be well advised to register with the **Data Protection Board**.

The Act defines a **data user** as being someone who makes use of **personal data** that is on a computer. Basically, personal data is data held about individuals. A **data subject** as defined by the Act is any person who has data about them on a computer. Such data on a computer has to be processed by the computer's software before it serves the purpose of information. It is this information that the Data Protection Registrar wants to know about.

Essentially, the data users must declare what information they have access to on a data subject and the uses to which they will put that information. The main objective of the Act is to ensure that individuals are aware of what is being held about them on business computers and to allow them access to this information. There are, however, many exemptions, such as medical records, criminal records and information deemed necessary to be kept secret in the national interest.

If a business is only using the Sales Ledger or Purchase Ledger for preparing and sending invoices and statements and does not use the comment details for a contact name, then registration may not be necessary. Also, if customers and suppliers are companies, and individuals cannot be identified in the data, registration is not necessary. In the same way with wages, if all a data user does with the data is to pay wages and prepare statutory returns, registration is not necessary.

If customer and supplier lists are used for sending out sales promotions, the data user must register. Likewise, if data on the payroll is used for management information about staff sickness or any form of staff monitoring.

Forms for registration are available at any main post office. These forms require the business to reveal the kind of data it holds on individuals and the purpose for which it wants to use it. The business must also give details on how data subjects can find out what data is held on computer about them.

In addition to the possible need to register, businesses must comply with certain practices with regard to holding personalised data on computer. These are:

1   Data must be obtained fairly and lawfully.
2   Data can only be used for the specified purpose set out in the original submission to the Registrar. If the business wishes to change the way it uses such data, then it must re-apply.
3   Data must not be disclosed to unauthorised parties. Again, authorised parties must be stated within the original application.
4   Data held must be adequate, relevant and not excessive for the purposes for which it is being held.
5   Data must be kept accurate and up to date. This principle should really apply to *all* data in an accounting system if the system is being managed and run properly.
6   Data must not be kept longer than is necessary.
7   Any 'data subject' must be allowed to see the data held on them in readable and legible form. This means businesses must have the mechanism for extracting a complete profile kept on an individual in the event that it is requested. If a data subject does approach a data user requesting such information, the data user can demand a fee to cover any administration costs.
8   A data user must have appropriate security against unauthorised access.

If a firm is in doubt, then it should always register (the cost of registration is small).

The information sent to the Registrar is available to any member of the public for inspection.

INSTALLING SAGE ON YOUR SYSTEM

Having acquired your hardware and Sage software, you need first to install it on your system. Many businesses purchasing a complete system might well have this done for them. However, it is not a bad idea to examine how it is installed as this will tell you something about the package.

The need to install a package on a system comes about because the package was not written for a specific system or for a specific business. The installation of the package will put the software on to your hard disk, which matches the computer system you are using and is set up for your type of business.

When your software is despatched it comes with:

a   a set of disks containing the applications software
b   an Installation guide
c   an Accounting user guide
d   a System Manager user guide

Before you start, establish the following on your system:

1   The drive name where floppy disks are entered, normally drive A
2   The hard drive location where Sage is to be installed. For most stand-alone systems this will normally be drive C:
3   The version of Sage which you have – *Bookkeeper, Accountant, Accountant Plus* or *Financial Controller*
4   The type of computer you have, eg an IBM or IBM compatible, Apricot or RM Nimbus
5   The type of printer you have
6   The number of customers for which your business wishes to open an account. This needs to relate to the number of customers you will sell to on a credit basis. Be generous with the number, to allow for rapid expansion without too much upheaval for the computer system. As a guide, assume twice as many as you need now. If you are following the examples in this book, you will need 50 customers
7   The number of businesses for which your business has suppliers' accounts. This is the number of suppliers who will supply you on a credit basis. Again, be generous with the number to allow for future new suppliers. If you are following the examples in this book, you will need 50 suppliers
8   The number of nominal accounts will also be asked for when Sage is installed. This refers to all the types of accounts covering business expenses (eg light and heat, motor expenses, stationery), and accounts covering the organisation's assets, its liabilities and more. This book in its examples allows for 100 such accounts. For a business starting off with the Sage package, seek advice from the accountant if unsure and, again,

be generous and enter a bigger number of accounts than is needed at present

With this information at hand, you are now ready to install your software.

Check your computer is plugged into the mains electricity circuit. Switch it on and wait for the operating system to load. (If you do not have a hard disk system, you will need to insert your operating system disk into disk drive A and follow the instructions for loading it.)

You will see on your screen the DOS prompt, usually C:, and at this point you should make a back-up copy of the disks you have received from Sage, as a precaution against anything going wrong. To do this refer to your computer Manual about how to make copies of disks.

Place the Sage disk labelled Installation into the drive. This should be in the drive known as A:

From the keyboard enter the command SAGELOAD

You will now be taken through a set of questions that Sage needs to ask to install the software correctly. Follow the screen instructions carefully. The whole process takes just a few minutes. As a result of the installation, you will have an applications package that is installed to be compatible with your computer hardware and capable of coping with your business needs.

2 The Sales Ledger

INTRODUCTION

This chapter starts us off with the Sage package by looking at the way it handles trading with the customers of a business. The purpose of a Sales Ledger is to help a business keep a good set of records about the dealings it has with its customers. When considering the use of the Sales Ledger, we are only concerned primarily with those customers who sell on a credit term basis rather than for cash.

For most of us going about our shopping, we would normally pay cash. From the business point of view, the retailer will not need the Sales Ledger for such a cash transaction. In practice, it is largely non-retailing businesses and retailing businesses that deal with mail order which need the Sales Ledger.

The Sales Ledger is a collection of customer accounts. Customers who deal with the business on this basis will normally order the goods and the business will deliver the goods and then send an invoice for payment. At a subsequent date, ranging from a few days to a few weeks, the customer will make a payment. The Sales Ledger will play a crucial role in managing the customer accounts. Those customers owing the business money are called **debtors** and are regarded by accountants as an **asset** to the business, as they will provide money to it.

At this point you ought to be aware of the documents used in sales transactions:

1   An **Invoice** is used to indicate to a customer what has been bought, how much has been bought and the amount it is costing the customer.

2   A **Credit Note** is used to *reduce* the amount the customer owes the business. Such a document is often issued when goods are returned to the business or the business decides to reduce the amount it wants its customer to owe.

There are more documents involved than this, but these are the two main ones for the purpose of getting to grips with the Sales Ledger in the first instance.

The Sales Ledger can be used just as effectively for services rendered as it can for goods sold (or a combination of both). Such facilities offered by a Sales Ledger must allow a user the ability to create, delete and amend customer details on the ledger, as well as record all transactions between the business and the customer.

Additional requirements would be a good report system on the Sales Ledger to ensure the business is aware of how much is owed to it and by whom. Another important function of the Sales Ledger for many businesses is to give information on VAT collected from sales.

Figure 2.1 gives an overview of the function of a Sales Ledger, with input activities showing the maintenance of customer records and entry of transactions data. The output activities will consist of the customer statements, audit trails and reports.

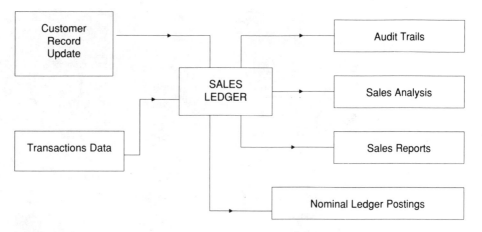

Fig. 2.1

An important requirement of a Sales Ledger is to provide details of sales, receipts and debtors to the **Nominal Ledger**. This will be dealt with in some length in Chapters 4 and 5.

In addition to supplying the organisation's needs, there is a requirement to supply information to those customers and clients to whom the organisation is selling. Such information may include details of invoices sent to them in the past and regular **statements of account**. A statement of account gives details of all transactions undergone with the firm over a specific period of time. Sage refers to these reports as transactions histories.

The Sage Sales Ledger section of the package will meet these requirements along with many others. There are other reporting facilities available for, in particular, management information which will be dealt with in a later chapter.

As a useful tip in operating a Sales Ledger, it is often a good idea to **batch process** much of the work. For example, when adding transactions to the Sales Ledger, it is often best to do a few at the same time (say weekly) rather than enter them to the ledger on an *ad hoc* basis (as each comes in). This will save both time and possible confusion caused by making a large number of visits to the computer to enter small amounts of transactions data.

The **audit trail** is a series of lists indicating all the data that has been entered into the Sales Ledger during a current period. This will be required for checking omissions and errors, and also for subsequent auditing purposes.

GETTING STARTED

If you have not installed your Sage package on to your computer, you will need to do so now by referring to Chapter 1. If your package has been installed, then you are ready to start. When you load Sage into your computer an opening screen similar to that shown in Fig 2.2 will be displayed for a few seconds.

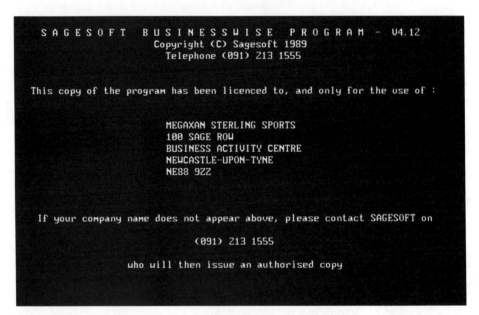

```
S A G E S O F T   B U S I N E S S W I S E   P R O G R A M  -  V4.12
                   Copyright (C) Sagesoft 1989
                   Telephone (091) 213 1555


   This copy of the program has been licenced to, and only for the use of :


              MEGAXAN STERLING SPORTS
              100 SAGE ROW
              BUSINESS ACTIVITY CENTRE
              NEWCASTLE-UPON-TYNE
              NE88 9ZZ



   If your company name does not appear above, please contact SAGESOFT on

                     (091) 213 1555

               who will then issue an authorised copy
```

Fig 2.2

The opening screen will reveal the address of your business or institution, along with details about Sagesoft. This confirms who is the owner of the package. Once the package has been purchased and then installed on your system, you have all that is needed to run Sage. You are advised, however, to register your ownership with Sage so that Sage can keep you updated with feature changes or on some issues such as changes in VAT. Also, some businesses may wish to use Sage as a source for purchasing stationery.

The next screen asks for both the **date** and a **password** (see Fig 2.3). The date revealed will be the date determined by your computer system. If you wish this changed, then you should enter the new date with six numbers in the format 'ddmmyy'. The password given by Sage can be changed using another program. If you have not altered this password, then it is likely to be **LETMEIN**. If this does not work, then you will need to consult your manual or the dealer who sold the package.

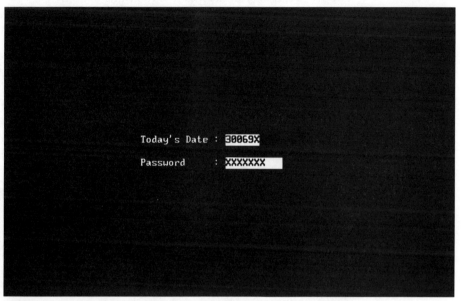

Fig 2.3

Once Sage is loaded and you have entered your password, you will see an opening **Sage Menu** such as the one in Fig 2.4.

A menu is a list of the options available to a user. The menu in Fig 2.4 is for Sage Bookkeeper. If you are using Accountant, Accountant Plus or

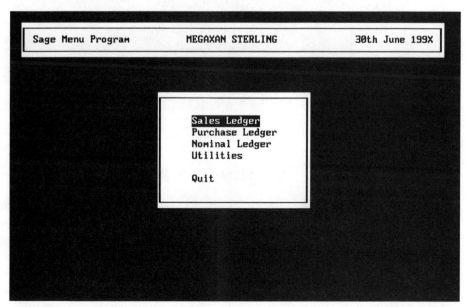

Fig 2.4

Financial Controller, you will have more options than this on your menu. Later chapters in this book will investigate these extra functions. At present we shall make use of those available to all Sage users. To select the Sales Ledger function, you need to highlight this option.

The **Up** and **Down** arrow keys on your keyboard allow you to select what option you require. Ensure **Sales Ledger** is highlighted and then press the **Enter** (or Return) key.

The next menu shows the activities available within the Sales Ledger function. To go back to the original menu, you need to press the **Esc key**. The Sage system is a hierarchy of menus, which allows an operator the facility of 'homing in' on the activity required by selecting the appropriate menu options. Fig 2.5 illustrates the structure of activities available in the Sales Ledger function.

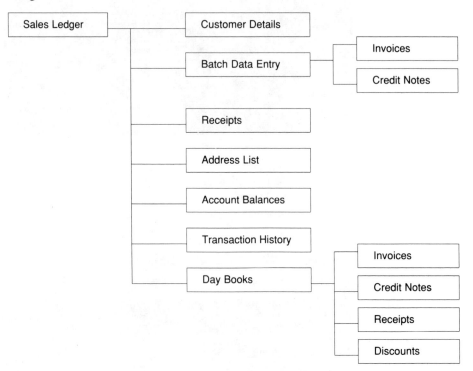

Fig 2.5

Figure 2.6 gives the menu of activities you can select from the Sales Ledger function.

Before you process any transactions, you will need to enter details of your customers. Such details will be used to build up a **database** of customers against which various transactions can be associated. In Chapter 1 you were told about installation. If you followed the suggested installation there, you have allowed for 50 customers.

Select **Customer Details** from the Sales Ledger menu (highlight with the arrow key and press **Enter** (Return)), to find yourself looking at a blank form

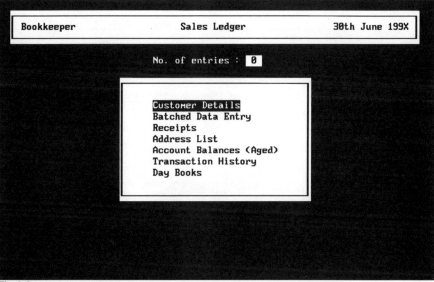

Fig 2.6

on the screen. The details, once entered into the form, will be stored as a customer **record** and give the **standing** (or **static**) details of a customer. In other words, details about a customer that only change infrequently.

Enter the Account reference as 0010. You will be asked if this is a new account. The computer is telling you that it cannot find a customer with such a reference and wants to know if you want a new one created. Answer **Yes** by highlighting this with the Right arrow key and press **Enter** (Return). Complete the form with the help of Fig 2.7.

Fig 2.7

Each line in the form will be stored as a **field**. Consequently, the customer **record** is a collection of 12 fields, as outlined in Fig 2.8.

Field numbers	Name	Purpose
1	Account reference	This has to be a **unique field,** because every customer must have a different field name. You can use numbers or letters or a mixture of both as a field name
2	Account name	This should be the customer's name
3–6	Address	Four address lines, usually the address where the invoices are sent
7	Credit limit	An amount that you are willing to let the customer owe you
8	Turnover	This shows the value of sales made to this customer over a period of time. It helps a business to get an idea of the customer's relative importance to the business
9	Telephone number	
10	Contact name	Who we can contact at the customer's business regarding sales and/or accounts
11	Discount code	This is linked with stock control but for now the D20 means this customer is allowed a discount of 20% of list price
12	Analysis code	This will be used to help us get an analysis of sales to customers

Fig 2.8

The field that holds the customer account reference is a **key field** in that it is the key that identifies the customer record. In order to achieve this, no two customers can have the same account reference, hence the concept of a unique field. It is quite acceptable for one customer to have more than one account with a business, which is often the case when the customer is a large corporation with many different departments.

When the form is complete, you should press the **Esc** key to inform the computer you have finished with the form. At the foot of the screen you are given four options:

Post   will create, or amend, the record for this customer
Edit   will allow you to stay with the form and make changes
Abandon   will leave the form and do nothing with the data
Delete   will delete the record from the database if it already exists

If you need to make any corrections, then highlight the **Edit** option with the arrow keys and press **Enter** (Return). You can move up and down the form with the respective arrow keys and re-enter text where the changes need to be made. If you make an error in the record once it has been saved or some details about the customer need altering, you can always return to the record and change the details at a later date.

When you are satisfied that the details are correct, select **Post** and press **Enter** (Return). Now key in some more customer records. The following list gives some suggestions, but you should add some of your own to gain the practice needed.

0010		0020	
Wantworth Cricket Club		Jackson General Sports	
The Sports Centre		100 High Street	
Hydean Way		Glasgow	
Perth			
Credit Limit	: 500	Credit Limit	: 300
Turnover	: 0	Turnover	: 0
Tel. No.	: 0999-3289103	Tel. No.	: 0901-2003
Contact Name	: Jo Blake	Contact Name	: Fred Draper
Discount Code	: D20	Discount Code	: D10
Analysis Code	: H200	Analysis Code	: H200

0030		0040	
Harriers Football Club		Dipple Store	
The Sports Centre		The Oval	
Hull		Manchester	
Credit Limit	: 300	Credit Limit	: 450
Turnover	: 0	Turnover	: 0
Tel. No.	: 0199-92921	Tel. No.	: 299231
Contact Name	: T J Kicker	Contact Name	: Bill
Discount Code	:	Discount Code	: D12.5
Analysis Code	: H100	Analysis Code	: H100

0050		0060	
Sports Super Centre		Howes Gym Centre	
Sports Arena		12 Spring Avenue	
London		Bexley	
Credit Limit	: 600	Credit Limit	: 300
Turnover	: 0	Turnover	: 0
Tel. No.	: 071-999-0010	Tel. No.	: 081-999-0021
Contact Name	: Mary or Jack	Contact Name	: Jane Brown
Discount Code	: D10	Discount Code	:
Analysis Code	: L100	Analysis Code	: L100

To finish entering customer records, press the **Esc** key when you have an empty form on screen.

Before you start entering transactions, it is worth obtaining from the computer a list of names and addresses. At this stage you should be back at the Sales Ledger menu. Select the option **Address List**. To see a list of ALL accounts on the screen, simply press **Enter** (Return) on the line 'Lower Account Reference' and repeat again for 'Upper Account Reference'. You are now being asked if you want a list of names or addresses. Names will give you a list of account references and their account names, while addresses gives both name and address.

On the last question you being asked how you want the list. You can select one of the following:

a **Printer**   A listing of the accounts is sent to the printer.
          Ensure the printer is on and prepared for printing.
b **Screen**   A listing of the accounts is scrolled on to the screen
          for inspection.
c **File**   A listing of the accounts is sent to a file on your data disk for
          printing at a later stage or use for word processing.

Controlling where information is output is a feature of the Sage package and you should try to become familiar with it as soon as possible.

Figure 2.9 shows a screen where all accounts are selected for names only.

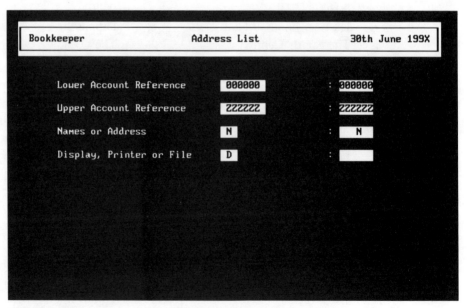

Fig 2.9

ENTERING TRANSACTION DATA

The activities in this section will involve entering details of invoices that have been sent to customers and also any credit notes. Before you can enter such details, you will need to make sure that the system is aware of the VAT rate to be charged. If a business is registered for VAT then it is obliged to charge its customers VAT and pass this sum on to HM Customs & Excise. At the time of writing the following VAT rates applied:

Zero rate on some items such as food and children's clothing
Standard rate of 17.5%
Exempt items

Zero rated items are those goods and services that our own Government chooses not to tax, while exempt items are those that cannot be taxed under EC regulations. It is up to a business to be aware of what items are subject to a charge for VAT. Most businesses will be aware of this from the outset. What is required for the purposes of running the Sage package is to let the computer be aware of this.

Return to the main Sage menu (see Fig 2.4) and select **Utilities**. Here you will see the **VAT Code Changes** options, which you should now select. The table that appears shows the default settings that Sagesoft had when the package was sold to you. To change the default settings, use the arrow keys to highlight the cells (the places where the figures appear which you wish to change) and then type in the correct numbers. In Fig 2.10 column 0 has been set with a column of zeros which is being used to store the zero rates. Column 1 shows 15.000 which has to be altered to 17.500 to change the standard rate of VAT to 17.5%.

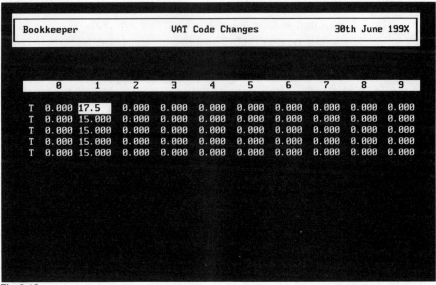

		0	1	2	3	4	5	6	7	8	9
Bookkeeper				VAT Code Changes					30th June 199X		
T		0.000	17.5	0.000	0.000	0.000	0.000	0.000	0.000	0.000	0.000
T		0.000	15.000	0.000	0.000	0.000	0.000	0.000	0.000	0.000	0.000
T		0.000	15.000	0.000	0.000	0.000	0.000	0.000	0.000	0.000	0.000
T		0.000	15.000	0.000	0.000	0.000	0.000	0.000	0.000	0.000	0.000
T		0.000	15.000	0.000	0.000	0.000	0.000	0.000	0.000	0.000	0.000

Fig 2.10

Throughout this book the following settings have been assumed:

T0   zero rated VAT
T1   standard rated VAT
T2   items exempt from VAT
T9   non-VAT transactions

Getting this right first time for a business is essential, as the reports at subsequent dates will form the basis of the VAT returns required by HM Customs & Excise.

When you are satisfied that the VAT settings are correct, press the **Esc** key to return to the Utilities menu. This will also store the new rates, if they have been changed.

Return to the main Sage menu and go back to the Sales Ledger function. By now you should be ready to enter some invoice details.

Entering invoices

From the Sales Ledger menu select **Batched Data Entry**. From here you can select either invoices (which will add to the amount owing to the business by a customer) or credit notes (reducing the amount owing to the business). Select **invoices** and an empty form will appear.

The system allows you to enter multiple invoices by using a single form, which can save time. An operator would normally have a batch of several invoices with details to enter.

A box under **A/C** should now be highlighted. It is asking for the account number of the customer whom you are invoicing. Enter 0010 in here and you will see the account name appear above to confirm that you are invoicing the right customer. If you use the **F4** function key, you can select the account required from a list of the accounts available.

The next column is asking for the **Date**. Sage helps you save time because, if you want to use the system date stored in your computer, you simply press the **F5** function key. The date that appears on the screen should be the date that appears on the invoice. Clearly, it would therefore be ideal if the date on the invoice was the same date as the day the invoice is entered into the computer.

The column **INV** is for the invoice number. In practice, a business will have a number unique to each invoice, usually going in number sequence.

The next column is asking for the **Nominal Code (N/C)**. When goods or services are invoiced to a customer, it is important that the sale is recorded in an appropriate Sales Account. Although this will be covered in Chapter 4, it is important to be aware of the need for nominal accounts to store such details. To help you, Sage allows you to scan through the nominal accounts available by pressing function key **F4** when you are ready to enter the nominal code. Figure 2.11 shows the list of accounts available.

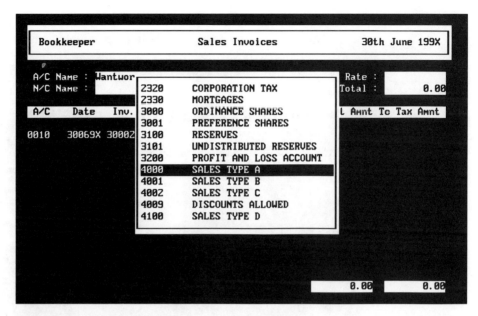

Fig 2.11

If you installed your software using the suggested layout of accounts (default) given by Sage, then account nominal numbers 4000, 4001, 4002, 4100 and 4101 are named as Sales A, Sales B, Sales C, Sales D and Sales E respectively. Although these may not be appropriate names for accounts, you are advised to use these for now. In Chapter 4 you will examine how these account names can be changed, how extra accounts can be added and how the layout can be altered. Using the Down and Up arrow keys you simply select the account to which the sales belong.

The next column headed **Dep** is used if a business has different departments and wants to attribute the sales to a particular department. For now, ignore the column by pressing the Enter (Return) key to display a value of 0. Another way that this column could be used is to record sales against different sales staff, where each salesperson is given a department number. This information is of use when extracting reports.

The **details** column simply describes what has been sold, or any other particulars the business wishes to record.

The **Nett** amount refers to the amount being charged to the customer *before* VAT is added. If the invoice only shows the Gross amount (total with VAT), then this can be entered and the computer can calculate the VAT and arrive at the Nett price.

Tc refers to the tax code which is shown as T0, T1, T2 or T9. When T1 is entered, the **Tax Amnt** column works out the VAT as though the figure in the Nett amount column is correct and the VAT has to be calculated on this figure. If the figure in the Nett column is the Gross amount, then pressing < key and **Shift** at the same time will recalculate the Nett column by subtracting the VAT from it and putting VAT into the VAT column.

Figure 2.12 shows a number of invoice entries. Try to enter these, along with some of your own, using the facilities available and mentioned here.

```
┌─────────────────────────────────────────────────────────────────────────┐
│ ┌─────────────────────────────────────────────────────────────────────┐ │
│ │ Bookkeeper                   Sales Invoices            30th June 199X │ │
│ └─────────────────────────────────────────────────────────────────────┘ │
│                                                                           │
│   A/C Name :  ┌──────────────────────────┐     Tax Rate :    │  17.500│  │
│   N/C Name :  │                          │     Batch Total : │ 1920.03│  │
│               └──────────────────────────┘                               │
│   A/C    Date    Inv.   N/C   Dep.     Details      Nett Amnt Tc Tax Amnt │
│                                                                           │
│   0010  30069X 300023 4000    0 Cricket Balls         30.00  T1    5.25   │
│   0010  30069X 300023 4001    0 Sports Bags           17.87  T1    3.13   │
│   0020  30069X 300024 4000    0 Cricket sets         220.00  T1   38.50   │
│   0020  30069X 300024 4001    0 Scarves               25.00  T1    4.38   │
│   0020  30069X 300024 4002    0 Soccer balls          40.00  T1    7.00   │
│   0030  30069X 300025 4002    0 Shirts & Shorts      468.09  T1   81.91   │
│   0040  30069X 300026 4000    0 Bat, Ball & Pads     320.00  T1   56.00   │
│   0050  30069X 300027 4000    0 Cricket Starter set   85.11  T1   14.89   │
│   0050  30069X 300027 4001    0 Hats, Scarves         88.00  T1   15.40   │
│   0060  30069X 300027 4001    0 Shirts & Shorts      340.00  T1   59.50   │
│                                                                           │
│                                                                           │
│   Do you want to : Post Edit Abandon         │ 1634.07│      │ 285.96│    │
└─────────────────────────────────────────────────────────────────────────┘
```

Fig 2.12

Once the invoice details are entered, you should press **Esc** and you will then be asked to select Post, Edit or Abandon. To **Abandon** at this stage will mean the whole form is ignored and lost. **Edit** allows you the chance to go through and make any corrections. To **Post** the entries means the invoice details are recorded against the respective customers and the sales amounts are posted to their respective nominal accounts.

Once you have posted the entries, a blank form reappears on the screen. You can either enter another batch of invoices or press **Esc** and return to the Batch Entry menu.

Entering Credit Notes

From the Batch Entry menu select the option **Credit Notes**. Entries here work exactly the same as those for invoices. Figure 2.13 shows two such entries.

The effect of a credit note is to reduce the amount owing by a customer. It also requires the amount of VAT on the items to be deducted and recorded separately. There could be a number of reasons why a credit note entry has to be made:

- Because a customer has returned goods. In this instance, you should use a Nominal Account for Goods Returned Inwards to distinguish it from simply a goods sale. In the example given in this chapter, it has been recorded in the Sales Account of the nominal ledger.

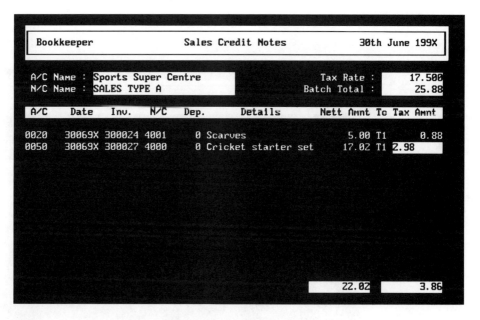

Bookkeeper			Sales Credit Notes			30th June 199X	

| A/C Name : Sports Super Centre | | | | | Tax Rate : | 17.500 |
| N/C Name : SALES TYPE A | | | | | Batch Total : | 25.88 |

A/C	Date	Inv.	N/C	Dep.	Details	Nett Amnt	Tc	Tax Amnt
0020	30069X	300024	4001	0	Scarves	5.00	T1	0.88
0050	30069X	300027	4000	0	Cricket starter set	17.02	T1	2.98
						22.02		3.86

Fig 2.13

- A subsequent discount might be offered for some reason.

- You may want to correct an overcharge to a customer or to counteract an invoice that should not have been done.

Whatever the reason for the credit note, the effect is to CREDIT the customer's account while at the same time you will DEBIT some nominal account. This compares with an invoice, which will DEBIT the customer's account while it CREDITS a sales nominal account.

Entering receipts

For any business to survive it will need to receive payment from its customers. The Sales Ledger, however, only addresses the issue of customers paying for goods they have had on credit. When a payment is received from a customer, it is used to settle outstanding invoices.

From the main Sales Ledger menu you should select the **receipts** option to enter payment details. Figure 2.14 shows an entry where customer 0010 has sent in a cheque for £40. You are first confronted with a screen that tells you the nominal code is 1200, which is the Bank Account reference given by Sage when it is installed with its own layout. Unless you want this changed, you should move to the **A/C Ref** and enter the account reference of the customer who has sent the cheque. Using the **F4** function key gives you a list to choose from. The narratives on the right-hand side of the screen simply remind you of the respective account names. The payment date will normally be the same as the computer date, which is entered by either typing in the numbers or using the **F5** key. The cheque number should be entered as it may prove useful in the event of future scrutiny.

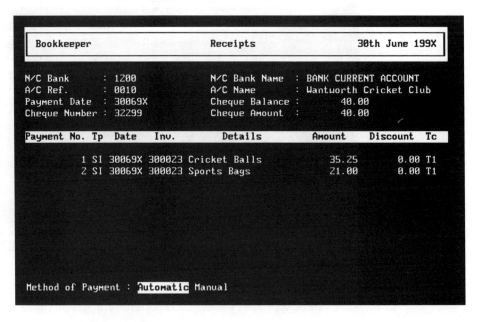

Fig 2.14

You will now be given the option of whether you want the cheque amount offset against invoices automatically or manually. By selecting **automatic**, the computer will start settling the longest outstanding invoices first. If there is insufficient money to settle an invoice, then it will be partly paid. In most cases, this is the normal practice when payments are received.

Figure 2.15 gives an example of a situation where the manual option has been selected. In this instance a cheque for £150 has been received and it has been decided to part pay three of the invoices and settle one of them in full. As you enter the amounts you will see the cheque amount in the top part of the screen remains as £150 and the cheque balance changes. The cheque balance should arrive at zero before you can **Post** the details to the customers' account and the nominal bank account.

The column headed **Tp** indicates the type of transaction being settled. **SI** indicates Sales Invoice, while **SC** indicates Sales Credit. When a Sales Credit is *settled*, it will increase the cheque balance, having the opposite effect to settling an invoice. A Sales Credit can therefore be used to part settle an invoice.

In Fig 2.16 you will see an example where the Credit Note issued to account 0020 has been settled in FULL, being balanced by PART settling a Sales Invoice. For these transactions, the bank account has been the nominal account where the amounts are recorded; a situation that is discussed further in Chapter 4.

```
┌────────────────────────────────────────────────────────────────────────┐
│ Bookkeeper                    Receipts                   30th June 199X  │
└────────────────────────────────────────────────────────────────────────┘

N/C Bank        : 1200        N/C Bank Name  : BANK CURRENT ACCOUNT
A/C Ref.        : 0020        A/C Name       : Jackson General Sports
Payment Date    : 30069X      Cheque Balance :      0.00
Cheque Number   : 200102      Cheque Amount  :    150.00

Payment No. Tp  Date    Inv.      Details       Amount    Discount  Tc

  PART    3 SI  30069X 300024 Cricket sets      158.50      0.00 T1
  PART    4 SI  30069X 300024 Scarves            23.38      0.00 T1
  FULL    5 SI  30069X 300024 Soccer balls        0.00      0.00 T1
  PART   11 SC  30069X 300024 Scarves             2.88      0.00 T1
```

Fig 2.15

```
┌────────────────────────────────────────────────────────────────────────┐
│ Bookkeeper                    Receipts                   30th June 199X  │
└────────────────────────────────────────────────────────────────────────┘

N/C Bank        : 1200        N/C Bank Name  : BANK CURRENT ACCOUNT
A/C Ref.        : 0020        A/C Name       : Jackson General Sports
Payment Date    : 30069X      Cheque Balance :      0.00
Cheque Number   : 099219      Cheque Amount  :      0.00

Payment No. Tp  Date    Inv.      Details       Amount    Discount  Tc

         3 SI  30069X 300024 Cricket sets      158.50      0.00 T1
  PART    4 SI  30069X 300024 Scarves           20.50      0.00 T1
  FULL   11 SC  30069X 300024 Scarves            0.00      0.00 T1
```

Fig 2.16

Before moving to the next section which will extract various reports, enter some more transactions in order to get some practice and to be able to extract more extensive reports later on.

EXTRACTING TRANSACTION REPORTS

From the Sales Ledger menu there are three more options not yet examined. These are Account Balances (Aged), Transactions History and Day Books, which are different ways of looking at the transactions you have entered.

Account balances (aged)

This is often referred to as an *Aged Debtors Report* and gives details of what amounts customers owe and how long they have been owing the money. Select the option **Account Balances (Aged)** from the Sales Ledger and examine the details on the screen.

You will be asked to state what accounts you want to examine. Pressing **Enter** to each suggestion of Lower Account '000000' and Upper Account 'ZZZZZZ' will list all accounts. The first screen gives details of the accounts and how much is outstanding. Pressing the **right arrow key** gives the Aged Analysis, similar to that shown in Fig 2.17.

```
┌──────────────────────────────────────────────────────────────────────┐
│ Bookkeeper            Account Balances (Aged)           30th June 199X │
└──────────────────────────────────────────────────────────────────────┘

  A/C      Balance     Current    30 Days    60 Days    90 Days    Older

 0010        16.25       16.25       0.00       0.00       0.00       0.00
 0020       179.00      179.00       0.00       0.00       0.00       0.00
 0030       550.00      550.00       0.00       0.00       0.00       0.00
 0040       376.00      376.00       0.00       0.00       0.00       0.00
 0050       183.40      183.40       0.00       0.00       0.00       0.00
 0060       399.50      399.50       0.00       0.00       0.00       0.00




Totals :   1704.15     1704.15       0.00       0.00       0.00       0.00

      Press  ESC  to finish,  RETURN  to continue,  ←  for Balance Summary
```

Fig 2.17

You will observe that the 30 Days, 60 Days, 90 Days and Older columns show zero. This is as a result of only having the current day's transactions in. Over time, figures will start appearing in the other columns.

It will always be in the best interests of a business to have its customers pay as soon as possible. While the debt is outstanding, the business is effectively lending its money to another firm. Such money can earn interest in the business's bank accounts or be used to reduce its own debt. Also, when a customer leaves a debt too long, there is the danger that the customer is in trouble and will not be able to pay at all. The dilemma faced for many businesses is that to press their customers too hard to settle early may lose trade with them.

Transactions history

This report allows you to examine the transactions undergone with any particular customer or group of customers. Figure 2.18 is such an example.

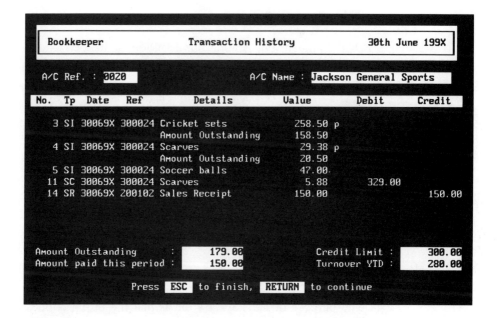

Fig 2.18

The number that appears in the first column is the transaction number. Each transaction you have entered will have been given a separate number in the sequence in which the transaction was carried out.

The second column indicates the transaction type. Three types are shown:

SI	Sales Invoice
SC	Sales Credit
SR	Sales Receipt

A fourth type not mentioned yet is:

SD	Sales Discount

The value column shows the value of the transaction. In the case of '300024 Cricket sets' the customer has been invoiced for £258.50 worth of goods, part of which has been paid, as indicated by the small 'p' next to the value. This has left £158.50 still to pay. Scarves have also been partly settled with £20.50 outstanding. The soccer balls have been paid for in full with nothing now outstanding. The arithmetic is:

		£
Value of goods sent	258.50 + 29.38 + 47 =	334.88
Less a credit note of		5.88
Nett balance		329.00
Less the amount paid		150.00
Total outstanding		179.00

Of the amount outstanding, the transactions history tells us that the customer owes:

		£
300024	Crickets sets	158.50
300024	Scarves	20.50
	Total	179.00

The figure that shows turnover to date is the amount of sales **less** the VAT that had to be added on:

	£
Nett goods year to date (YTD)	280
VAT @ 17.5%	49
Gross	329

The purpose of leaving VAT out is that the business does not keep the VAT. The VAT will have to be passed on to HM Customs & Excise. Therefore, as far as the business is concerned, it has sold goods that give it a sales revenue of £280.

Such reports can be sent to customers on a regular basis, such as monthly, in the form of a customer statement of account and are a useful reminder to customers of what they owe.

Day Books

Select this option from the Sales Ledger, and you will see four further options, of which three enable you to extract a report. The **Sales Invoices** option will give a list of all invoices entered in the order in which you put them in. The options **Credit notes**, **Discounts** and **Receipts** work in exactly the same way.

In a business not using a computer it is customary to keep a book called a Sales Day Book, which is used to record details of each invoice issued. It is also used to record both receipts and credit notes. Such books are essential also to running a computerised accounts system and it is well worth producing a printout of each of these day books periodically for future reference.

DISCOUNTS

It was mentioned earlier in this chapter that it is not in the best interests of a business to allow customers to settle accounts too far into the future. Rather than issue threatening letters or impolite inferences on invoices, many businesses offer settlement discounts to their customers for settling early.

In the event of discounts being offered under such circumstances, you would enter these amounts when you record a sales receipt. When you examine purchases in the next chapter, you will see further how this works.

It is worth noting at this stage that allowing cash discounts in this fashion is quite distinct from offering a trade discount. A trade discount is normally offered to another firm in the trade which buys large quantities. Such trade discounts will result in the invoice amount being lower in the first instance. Consequently, you should enter the amounts into the computer AFTER the trade discounts have been allowed for. This is important as the invoice amount (with VAT) is an indication of what is owed by the customer.

Conclusion and exercises

Some important issues raised in this chapter have been covered lightly because they require a knowledge of other parts of the package. Some further issues regarding the Sales Ledger will be raised in later chapters.

As a way of gaining practice, you should try the following tasks:

1 Create at least 12 new customer accounts
2 Generate for each customer at least two invoices
3 Generate for four of your customers two credit notes
4 Receive a payment from five of your customers
5 Produce the following transactions reports
   a List of Invoices and Credit Notes
   b List of Receipts
6 Produce Transactions Histories on two accounts
7 Produce an Aged Debtors list
8 Produce a list of accounts and addresses
9 Determine the Outstanding Debtors Total

Note: It is not essential to produce printer listings of all of these, but simply to be able to access such information. In other words, a listing to the screen will suffice.

3 The Purchase Ledger

INTRODUCTION

Having now worked with the Sales Ledger, you will find that the Purchase Ledger looks fairly similar with a common set of keystrokes. The purpose of a Purchase Ledger is to record and help manage all purchases from suppliers.

When you dealt with the Sales Ledger, you only concerned yourself with trading sales, namely your customers. You will need to use the Purchase Ledger for all purchases made on a credit term basis.

The purchase ledger can be used just as effectively for services acquired as it can for goods bought (or a combination of both). As depicted in Fig 3.1, facilities offered by a Purchase Ledger must include allowing a user to create, delete or amend suppliers' details on the ledger as well as to record all transactions between the business and supplier. Additional requirements would be good reporting on the Purchase Ledger to ensure the business is keeping within defined budgets and is not building too much expensive debt. Controlling expenditure will always be an important part of business management and, although an efficient Purchase Ledger will not, by itself, control expenditure, the system should be capable of reporting any problems quickly so they can be rectified. Another important requirement of the Purchase Ledger to many businesses is to assist them in offering information on VAT collected from their sales.

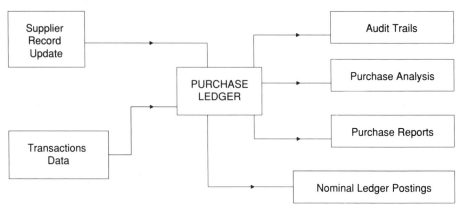

Fig 3.1

In general, purchases can fall into one of three categories:

a Purchases for trading, such as the purchase of raw materials that will go into stock for future manufacturing purposes, or purchases of stock for later resale.

b Purchases related to business expenses, such as stationery, electricity, rates and general office supplies. Such purchases will make up the overhead expenses of running a business.

c Capital purchases such as new buildings, delivery vans or the purchase of fixtures and fittings.

Other categories may also be identified, dependent on the particular type of business. Regardless of the type and nature of a purchase, the Purchase Ledger will treat them all in exactly the same way. The category of goods or services purchased will have to be considered when invoice details are entered to the ledger, and when purchase details need to be recorded in the nominal accounts.

The Purchase Ledger, in many ways, has an inverted function to that of the Sales Ledger. In other words, its function is almost the same as the Sales Ledger, but goods and services enter the business and payments result in money leaving the business bank accounts. The effect will be that the nominal accounts which record the purchases coming into the business will be *debited* by the purchase value while the Purchase Ledger Accounts which record the suppliers who they have been purchased from will be *credited* by the purchase value.

The activities within the Purchase Ledger are similar to those of the Sales Ledger. The structure of activities is virtually identical and it is a good idea at this stage to compare the few differences by examining Fig 3.2.

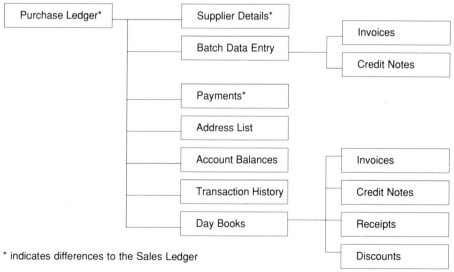

* indicates differences to the Sales Ledger

Fig 3.2

As a useful tip in operating the Purchase Ledger, it is often a good idea to **batch process** much of the work. For example, when adding transactions to the Purchase Ledger, it is often best to do a few at the same time (say weekly) rather than enter them to the ledger on an *ad hoc* basis. This will save both time and possible confusion.

At the end of each accounting period (usually monthly) there will be an **end-of-period** summarising activity, which will be examined in a later chapter. This will be necessary to ensure accounts do not get unnecessarily large as well as supplying important information needed by the business. (You will also perform the end-of-period activity for the Sales Ledger.)

As an important point, do not destroy or dispose of any supplier's invoices. Once their details have been entered to the computer, such documents should be filed in a safe place in case they are required for future reference; and a good number of them always will be.

As a final point in this introduction, you will not be required to enter any cash purchases through the Purchase Ledger. It will work in much the same as the Sales Ledger in that any cash transactions will be entered through the Nominal Ledger. Consequently, you will only be addressing the issue of purchases with suppliers that are made on a credit basis.

GETTING STARTED

Before you process any transactions with suppliers, you will need to enter details of your suppliers. Such details will be used to build up a **database** of suppliers against which various transactions can be associated. If you followed the suggested installation given in Chapter 1, you have allowed for 50 suppliers.

Select **Suppliers Details** from the Purchase Ledger menu, to find yourself looking at a blank form on the screen. The details, once entered into the form, will be stored as a supplier **record**, and give the **standing** (or **static**) details of a supplier. In other words, details about a supplier that only change infrequently such as their address. This compares with the **non-standing** (or **dynamic**) transactions data on each purchase, entered on a regular basis.

The fields that make up supplier records are similar to those of the customer records in the Sales Ledger. The field that holds the Supplier Account number is a **key field** in that it is the key that identifies the supplier record. In order to achieve this, no two suppliers can have the same account number. It may be possible that a supplier to a business is also a customer. In this event, an account in each ledger is needed.

Account numbers in the Purchase Ledger can be the same as those in the Sales Ledger. However, this is unwise at it could cause some confusion at a later stage.

Figure 3.3 shows a completed form for a supplier.

```
┌─────────────────────────────────────────────────────────────────┐
│ Bookkeeper              Supplier Details           17th July 199X │
└─────────────────────────────────────────────────────────────────┘


              Account Reference : P0010

                 Account Name : Ideal Sportswear plc
                      Address : 120 Spring Gardens
                           ..  : Hillingsworth
                           ..  : Northampton
                           ..  : NN22

                 Credit Limit :      500.00
                     Turnover :        0.00

                Telephone No. : 293912
                 Contact Name : Jackie Small
                Discount Code : D30
                Analysis Code : HOME


  Do you want to : Post Edit Abandon Delete
```

Fig 3.3

The supplier code is prefixed with a 'P' to illustrate that letters and numbers or a combination of both can be used. The 'P' has been used to illustrate that the account belongs to a supplier; there would be some logic in prefixing all Sales Ledger accounts in the same way with an 'S'.

The credit limit is imposed on the business by a supplier and should be known by the business. If no such credit limit exists, then this should be left blank. When the credit limit is reached, it would normally mean that the business is unable to receive more from this supplier until a payment is made to bring the balance to within the credit limit.

All the other fields work in exactly the same way as those of the Sales Ledger. At this stage, you should enter some supplier accounts so that you have something constructive to work with. The list shown here gives some suggestions.

P0010	P0020
Ideal Sportswear plc	James & Nichols plc
120 Spring Gardens	1 Hayley Common
Hillingsworth	Stevenage
Northampton	Herts
NN22	SS2 1EB

Credit Limit	500	Credit Limit	300
Turnover	0.00	Turnover	0
Telephone No	293912	Telephone No	932291
Contact Name	Jackie Small	Contact Name	David
Discount Code	D30	Discount Code	D25
Analysis Code	HOME	Analysis Code	HOME

P0030
Sports Supplies Inc
Runners Square
New York 2000
USA

Credit Limit   1000
Turnover   0.00
Telephone No
Contact Name
Discount Code
Analysis Code USA

P0050
Odessa Sports
The Square
Adelaide
South Australia

Credit Limit   1000
Turnover   0.00
Telephone No   010-209300111
Contact Name   Kevin
Discount Code D40
Analysis Code AUSTRALIA

P0040
Minerva Football Co Ltd
Metro Centre
St Albans Rd
St Albans AL5 0BY

Credit Limit   800
Turnover   0
Telephone No.   29991
Contact Name   John or Richard
Discount Code D20
Analysis Code HOME

P0060
Crazy Sporting World
Main Square
Calcutta
India

Credit Limit   500
Turnover   0
Telephone No   010-00292101
Contact Name   Mr Singh
Discount Code D25
Analysis Code INDIA

Before you start entering transactions, it is worth obtaining from the computer a list of names and addresses. You will need to be in the main Purchase Ledger menu and from here select the option **Address List**. To see a list of all supplier accounts on the screen, simply press **Enter** (Return) on the line 'Lower Account Reference' and repeat again for 'Upper Account Reference'.

You are now being asked if you want a list of names or addresses. Names will give you a list of account references and their account names while addresses gives both name and address. The final question asks how you want the list: on the screen as a Display (D), on your Printer (P), or sent to a File (F).

Help

At this point it is worth examining the availability of help within the Sage system. If you press function key **F1** you will see a screen of information similar to that shown in Fig 3.4.

The help screens will give you some details about what to do at any stage and certainly serve as a very good memory jogger if you have forgotten how

```
┌─────────────────────────────────────────────────────────────────┐
│ ┌───────────────────────────────────────────────────────────┐   │
│ │ Sage Help : 028        Supplier Details      17th July 199X │   │
│ └───────────────────────────────────────────────────────────┘   │
│                                                                   │
│ ┌───────────────────────────────────────────────────────────┐   │
│ │ Use [UP-ARROW] and [DOWN-ARROW] to move between fields      │   │
│ │ ----------------------------------------------------------- │   │
│ │ Turnover will be altered automatically as transactions are  │   │
│ │ entered onto each account.                                  │   │
│ │                                                             │   │
│ │ The discount code must be A, B, C or D followed by a number │   │
│ │ in the range 0 - 99                                         │   │
│ │ The A,B,C relates to discount rates recorded with the stock │   │
│ │ codes.                                                      │   │
│ │ ----------------------------------------------------------- │   │
│ │ Press [ESC] to exit from this option.                       │   │
│ │ Select POST to record new information, EDIT to make more    │   │
│ │ changes                                                     │   │
│ │ Select ABANDON to ignore new changes, DELETE will appear    │   │
│ │ if relevant.                                                │   │
│ │ ----------------------------------------------------------- │   │
│ │  F1  │ F2 │ F3 │ F4    │ F5 │ F6 │ F7 │ F8    │ F9 │ F10    │   │
│ │ Help │Pop-│    │ Quick │    │    │    │ Clear │    │        │   │
│ │      │Calc│    │ Ref   │    │    │    │ Field │    │        │   │
│ └───────────────────────────────────────────────────────────┘   │
└─────────────────────────────────────────────────────────────────┘
```

Fig 3.4

to perform a certain task. There are different help screens according to where you are in the package. If, for example, you are about to enter details for a supplier and press the help key (F1), the help screen will be related to that particular topic. Such help screens have now become a feature of software packages because computer memory has become big enough to store such details.

ENTERING TRANSACTION DATA

The activities in this section will require you to enter details of invoices and credit notes that have been received from suppliers. Before you can enter such details, you will need to make sure that the system is aware of the rate of VAT that has been charged. As the VAT was set when you worked with the Sales Ledger, there will be no need to enter these details again. If a business is registered for VAT then it is obliged to charge its customers VAT and pass this on to HM Customs & Excise. With respect to purchasing, the business will be paying out VAT. In this event, the business can claim this VAT back from HM Customs & Excise.

Transactions processing will involve entering a whole series of transactions. Each transaction will be stored in the computer as a transactions record. As with supplier records, a transaction record has its own structure. Figure 3.5 outlines such a record structure that consists of nine fields. Exactly the same transaction records structure exists with the Sales Ledger. When reports are extracted, you will often be given a report that is a compilation of more than one set of records.

Field numbers	Name	Purpose
1	Account reference	Account reference of the supplier on which the transaction is to be carried out
2	Transaction type	Invoice, Credit Note, etc
3	Date	Date of transaction
4	Document No	For example invoice number
5	Nominal code	The number of the Nominal Account to which the transaction gets posted, e.g. stock purchases account
6	Details	Any special information needed
7	Nett amount	Value of transaction before VAT
8	Tax amount	T0, T1, or T9
9	Tax amount	Amount of VAT

Fig 3.5

Entering Invoices

From the Purchase Ledger menu select **Batched Data Entry**. From here you can select either invoices or credit notes. Select **invoices** and an empty form will appear.

As with the Sales Ledger, the system allows you to enter multiple invoices via a single form, which can save time. When working on this activity, it would normally be the case that an operator has a set of invoices to work from with the details to enter.

A box under the **A/C** should now be highlighted. It is asking for the supplier account number of the supplier who has sent the invoice. Press function key **F4** and select a supplier. The next column is asking for the **Date**. Sage helps you save time because if you want to use the system date stored in your computer, you simply press the **F5** function key. The date that appears on the screen should be the date that appears on the invoice. The column **INV** is for the invoice number, which the supplier will have given.

The next column is asking for the **Nominal Code (N/C)**. It is at this point that you will need to be careful about what is being purchased. Buying, for example, goods for stock will have to be entered into a different Nominal Account to buying capital equipment for the business. In order to avoid any complications at this early stage, you are advised to enter all purchases into a purchases account set by Sage as account 5001. As before, pressing function key **F4** allows you to select the account from a list.

The next column headed **Dep** is used if a business has different departments and wants to attribute the purchase to a particular department or person. The **details** column is simply to describe what has been purchased or any other particulars the business wishes to record.

The **Nett** amount refers to the amount being charged by the supplier *before* VAT is added. If the invoice only shows the gross amount (total with VAT), then this can be entered and the computer can calculate the VAT and arrive at the nett price.

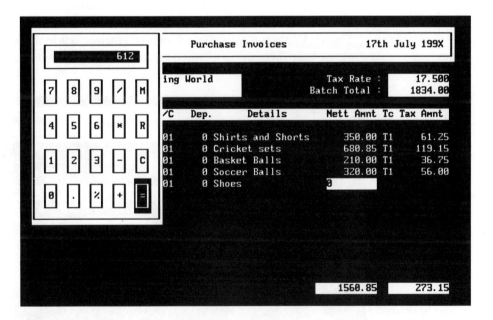

Fig 3.6

At this point it is worth investigating the calculator function by pressing function key **F2**. Figure 3.6 shows how it can be used to help calculate the nett amount.

Calculator

The calculator has been used to determine 51 times 12. To get to this you should, after pressing **F2**, enter the formula **12*51=** which is read as '12 times 51 equals' and reveals the figure 612. Simply press **Enter** and the figure is entered into the form where the cursor is positioned.

The screen calculator works just like a pocket calculator and allows the use of brackets. The mathematical symbols are:

+   for addition
−   for subtraction
*   for multiplication
/   for division

Tc refers to the tax code, which is given as T0, T1, T2 or T9, as you used in Chapter 2 for the Sales Ledger. When T1 is entered, the **Tax Amnt** column works out the VAT as though the figure in the Nett amount is correct and the VAT has to be calculated on this figure. If the figure in the Nett column is the gross amount, then pressing < key and **Shift** at the same time will recalculate the Nett column by removing the VAT on it and putting VAT into the VAT column.

Figure 3.7 shows a number of invoice entries. Try to enter these along with some of your own, using the facilities available and mentioned here.

```
┌─────────────────────────────────────────────────────────────────────┐
│ Bookkeeper              Purchase Invoices           28th July 199X    │
│                                                                       │
│ A/C Name :                                  Tax Rate :      17.500    │
│ N/C Name :                                  Batch Total :  2681.00    │
│                                                                       │
│ A/C     Date    Inv.   N/C   Dep.    Details      Nett Amnt Tc Tax Amnt│
│                                                                       │
│ P0010  17079X 002891 5001     0 Shirts and Shorts   350.00 T1   61.25 │
│ P0020  17079X 19291  5001     0 Cricket sets        680.85 T1  119.15 │
│ P0030  17079X 800121 5001     0 Basket Balls        210.00 T1   36.75 │
│ P0040  17079X 7118   5001     0 Soccer Balls        320.00 T1   56.00 │
│ P0060  17079X 61162  5001     0 Shoes               612.00 T9    0.00 │
│ P0030  15079X 800182 5001     0 Rugby Balls         200.00 T1   35.00 │
│                                                                       │
│ Do you want to : Post Edit Abandon        2372.85       308.15        │
└─────────────────────────────────────────────────────────────────────┘
```

Fig 3.7

Once the invoice details are entered, you should press the **Esc** key and you will then be asked to select Post, Edit or Abandon. To **Abandon** at this stage will mean the whole form is ignored and lost. **Edit** allows you the chance to go through and make any corrections. To **Post** the entries means the invoice details are recorded against the respective suppliers and the purchase nett amounts are posted to their respective nominal accounts.

Once you have posted the entries, a blank form reappears on the screen.

You can either enter another batch of invoices or press **Esc** and return to the Batch Entry menu.

Entering Credit Notes

From the batch entry menu select the other option of **Credit Notes**. Entries here work exactly the same as for invoices. Try making one or two entries before carrying on.

The effect of a credit note is to reduce the amount owing to a supplier. It may also require deducting VAT on these items and recording this separately.

The effect of a credit note is to DEBIT the supplier's account while at the same time you will CREDIT some nominal account. This compares with a purchase invoice which will CREDIT the supplier's account while it DEBITS a nominal account.

Paying suppliers

In paying suppliers for goods and services received, you will need to bear in mind any discounts offered for prompt payment, as well as the terms under which the purchases were made. For most businesses, good relations with their suppliers can be as important as good relations with customers. This is particularly so when dealing with suppliers who are specialists in their field or who offer generous discounts and/or credit terms. It may also be true for many manufacturing firms who work with low stocks of materials and rely for continuous production on efficient and reliable deliveries from their suppliers.

When making a payment via the Purchase Ledger, you are settling outstanding invoices with suppliers. The effect will be to debit a supplier account with the payment and credit the bank account of your business with the payment.

From the main Purchase Ledger menu you should select the **payments** option to enter such details. You are first presented with a screen that tells you the nominal code is 1200, which is the Bank Account reference given by Sage when it is installed with its own layout. Unless you want this changed, you should go to **A/C Ref** and enter the account reference of the supplier to whom you are sending a cheque. Using the **F4** function key gives you a list to choose from. The narratives on the right-hand side of the screen simply remind you of the respective account names. The payment date will normally be the same as the computer date, which is entered either by typing in the day/month/year numbers or using the **F5** key. The cheque number should be entered for future reference.

You will now be given the option of whether you want the cheque amount offset against invoices automatically or manually. By selecting **automatic**, the computer will start settling the longest outstanding invoices first. If there is insufficient money to settle an invoice, then it will be partly paid. If you choose the **manual** option, then you are given the choice as to which invoices you want fully or partly to pay.

The column headed **Tp** indicates the type of transaction being settled. **PI** indicates **Purchase Invoice**, while **PC** indicates **Purchase Credit**. When a Purchase Credit is *settled* it will have the opposite effect on the cheque balance to settling an invoice, in that it increases the balance. Settling a Purchase Credit should be used when you wish to part settle an invoice.

Entering a cash discount

Many suppliers may offer some cash incentive to a business for prompt payment, such as a percentage discount from an invoice amount owing if it is settled within 30 days. This has to be entered into the accounts as it has the effect of reducing the amount owing to the supplier. The principle, therefore, is to debit the supplier's account by the discount amount, in the same way as though this sum had been paid.

When you are entering a discount, you should first use the payment procedure to pay that part of the invoice that is being paid. After this, you should return to the payment screen and, instead of entering details of the cheque payment, use the discount option to settle the invoice.

In Figure 3.8 you will see that account P0020 has just one invoice left to settle which has an outstanding balance on it of 12. Using the payments option in the Purchase Ledger, you should enter details as though it is a payment, leaving cheque amount at zero, because we do not want to credit the bank account.

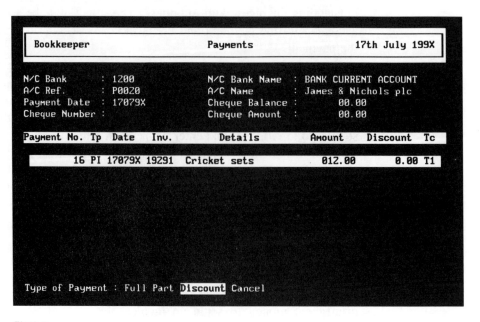

Fig 3.8

Select the **manual** method of payment and highlight the invoice to settle (there is only one in Figure 3.8). While the invoice record is highlighted, press **Enter** (Return) and then select **discount** option. You will now be asked to enter an amount. Press the **Esc** key to indicate that the invoice is to be settled. Finally, you should enter the tax code. In a business you will need to be aware of what discount codes should be entered. For this exercise enter **T1** and press **Enter** (Return). Figure 3.9 shows what the resulting transactions record should look like.

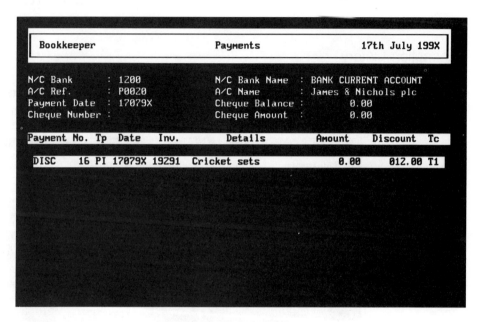

Fig 3.9

The Amount column has nothing in it, but the Discount column shows that £12 has been paid to settle the invoice, with DISC being shown in the payment column to confirm the transaction is a discount. Meanwhile, the top of the screen shows no cheque balance or cheque amount. You simply need to press **Esc** followed by **Post** to send these details to their respective accounts.

Before moving to the next section, which will extract various reports, you should enter some more transactions in order to get more practice and be able to extract extensive reports later on.

EXTRACTING TRANSACTION REPORTS

From the Purchase Ledger menu there are three more options not yet examined in this chapter. Account Balances (Aged), Transaction History and Day Books, which work in the same way as they did for the Sales Ledger.

Account balances (aged)

This is often referred to as an *Aged Creditors Report* and gives details of what we owe suppliers and how long the debt has been owing. Select this option from the Purchase Ledger menu and examine the details on the screen.

The value of these outstanding debts is referred to as *trade creditors* by accountants and appears on a company's balance sheet under the heading current liabilities. This compares with the customers' debts known as *trade debtors*, the value of which appear on the balance sheet under the heading current assets.

Transaction history

This report allows you to examine the transactions undergone with any particular supplier or group of suppliers. Figure 3.10 is such an example.

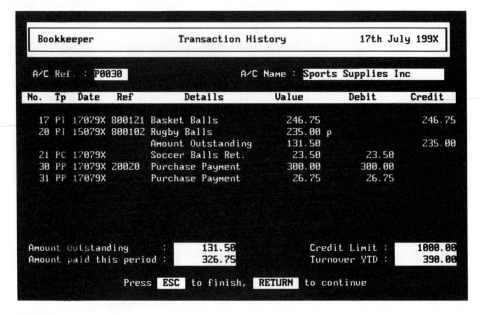

Fig 3.10

The number that appears in the first column is the transaction number. Each transaction you have entered will have been given a separate number in the sequence in which the transaction was carried out. These numbers also include all the Sales Ledger transactions and will form the basis of the audit trail later.

The second column indicates the transaction type. Three are shown:

PI   Purchase Invoice
PC   Purchase Credit
PP   Purchase Payment

A fourth type not appearing in this transaction history is:

PD   Purchase Discount

The value column shows the value of the transaction. In the case of '800102 Rugby Balls' the supplier has invoiced us for £235 worth of goods for which part of it has been paid as indicated by the small 'p' next to the value. This has left £131.50 still to pay. The basket balls have been paid for with nothing now outstanding. The arithmetic is:

			£
Value of goods received	246.75 + 235	=	481.75
Less a credit note of			23.50
Nett balance			458.25
Less the payments made	300 + 26.75		326.75
Total outstanding			131.50

Day Books

In this option of the Purchase Ledger, you will see four further options. The Purchase invoices option will give a list of all invoices entered in the order in which you put them in. Credit notes, Receipts and Discounts work in exactly the same way.

BACKING UP YOUR DATA

When you leave the Sage package from the main front (main) menu, you are asked if you wish to back up your data files. If you answer 'yes' to this question, the data files where the accounts information for your business is held, are copied on to another disk for safe-keeping. In the event of anything going wrong with the computer system in the future, the information can be restored to the state it was in when it was backed up.

For a business using a computer fairly regularly, it may be prudent to back up daily. For heavy users of computers, it might make sense to back up twice daily or more.

When finishing a session, if you answer **Yes** to the question 'Do you want to back up your data files?', the system will come up with a screen similar to the one shown in Figure 3.11.

The two lines under the headings 'Company, Date and Time' in the highlighted bar indicate when the last backups were made. From Fig 3.11 it can be seen that two previous backups have been made on Wednesday July 10 at 12.50 pm and on Wednesday July 17 at 12.51 pm. If your screen shows no such information, it means you have not yet backed up at all.

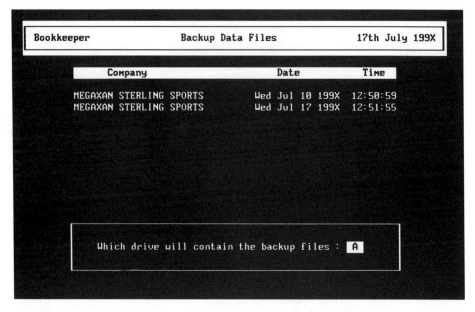

Fig 3.11

The next question asks where you want the backup information stored. If you choose A or B drive, then you are usually required to insert a floppy disk into that drive for the backup data to be stored. Select the drive where you want the information stored and, if appropriate, insert a formatted floppy disk into that drive, and press **Enter** (Return).

You will now see a series of file names displayed on the screen indicating what data files are being backed up.

More on backing up and restoration procedures will be examined in Chapter 9 when Sage Utilities are discussed.

Conclusion and exercises

Some important issues raised in this chapter have been covered lightly because they require a knowledge of other parts of the package. Some further issues regarding the Purchase Ledger will be raised in later chapters.

As a way of gaining practice, you should try the following tasks:

1   Create at least six new supplier accounts
2   Generate for each supplier at least two invoices
3   Generate for two of your suppliers one credit note each
4   Make some form of payment to three of your suppliers
5   Produce a full list of transactions showing:
   a   List invoices and credit notes
   b   List payments made
6   Produce Transactions Histories on two accounts
7   Produce an Aged Creditors List
8   Produce a list of accounts and addresses

9 Determine the Outstanding Creditors Total that would appear on the balance sheet as total creditors

10 Leave the Sage package and back up your accounts data

Note: It is not essential to produce printer listings of all of these, but simply to be able to access and examine such information. In other words, listings to the screen will suffice.

4 The Nominal Ledger

INTRODUCTION

The Nominal Ledger is used to record all dealings involving, on one side, assets of the firm such as buildings, stock and work in progress and, on the other side, how these assets have been financed. The financing of a business will be done either by its creditors or by those who own it. Apart from recording the financing of assets, the Nominal Ledger will need to record all the overheads of the business as well any income generated. In addition to this, the Nominal Ledger will be used to indicate the status of various accounts, as well as to produce profit statements and statements of the assets, liabilities and capital invested in the business. In essence, the Nominal Ledger records in some form all the financial transactions, a few of which you will have already come across. See Fig 4.1.

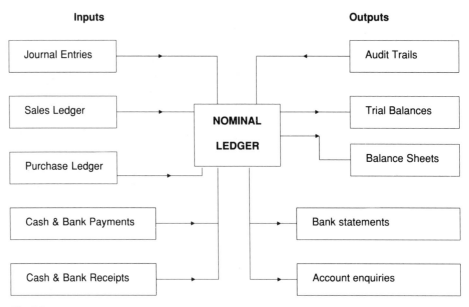

Fig 4.1

In Chapters 2 and 3 you worked with the Sales and Purchases Ledgers, from which you have already posted a considerable amount to the Nominal Ledger. Each time, for example, a sale was recorded, an amount was entered into one of the Sales Accounts in the Nominal Ledger to record goods being sold. Also, when a payment was received, the bank account in the Nominal Ledger was updated to record this fact.

The Nominal Ledger, by its very nature, is the cornerstone of an accounting system as, in varying forms, all business transactions will pass through it. It is worth noting that all business transactions do not necessarily involve money, as we have already seen. The Nominal Ledger uses the principle of **double entry**, a process whereby any transaction entered to the Nominal Accounts must have both a source account and destination account (credit and debit). As you work through this chapter and the remaining ones, it is hoped you will gain a good understanding of this principle. However, a knowledge of double entry bookkeeping beforehand will help you.

LOOKING AT DOUBLE ENTRY

In order to understand the principle of double entry in practical terms, you already have the opportunity to explore the entries made into the Nominal Ledger from your work undertaken in the previous two chapters. Start off by entering into the Nominal Ledger from the main Sage menu.

One of the first Nominal Accounts that can be checked is the Bank Account. Select from the Nominal Ledger menu the option **Control Account History** and then select **Bank Account.** Here you will see a list of bank transactions. Figure 4.2 illustrates such an account.

```
┌─────────────────────────────────────────────────────────────────────────┐
│ ┌─────────────────────────────────────────────────────────────────────┐ │
│ │ Bookkeeper              Bank Accounts              26th July 199X    │ │
│ └─────────────────────────────────────────────────────────────────────┘ │
│                                                                           │
│   A/C Ref. : 1200              A/C Name : BANK CURRENT ACCOUNT            │
│                                                                           │
│  ┌────┬────┬──────┬──────┬───────────┬────────┬─────────┬─────────┐      │
│  │No. │ Tp │ Date │ Ref  │  Details  │ Value  │  Debit  │ Credit  │      │
│  └────┴────┴──────┴──────┴───────────┴────────┴─────────┴─────────┘      │
│    13  SR  30069X 32299  Sales Receipt    40.00    40.00                  │
│    14  SR  30069X 20010Z Sales Receipt   150.00   150.00                  │
│    22  PP  17079X 20001  Purchase Payment 600.00            600.00        │
│    24  PP  17079X        Purchase Payment  50.00             50.00        │
│    25  PP  17079X 20002  Purchase Payment 300.00            300.00        │
│    26  PP  17079X 20005  Purchase Payment 230.00            230.00        │
│    27  PP  17079X 20010  Purchase Payment 500.00            500.00        │
│    29  PP  17079X        Purchase Payment  40.00             40.00        │
│    30  PP  17079X 20020  Purchase Payment 300.00            300.00        │
│    31  PP  17079X        Purchase Payment  26.75             26.75        │
│                                                                           │
│                                         Totals  :  190.00   2046.75       │
│                                         Balance :           1856.75       │
│                                                                           │
│          Press  ESC  to finish,  RETURN  to continue                      │
└─────────────────────────────────────────────────────────────────────────┘
```

Fig 4.2

In the **Tp** column, Figure 4.2 shows how the transactions were entered. **SR** is Sales Receipt and **PP** Purchase Payment, as described for you in the details column. At this stage, it is worth getting to grips with which figures were entered into the Debit column and which into the Credit column. You should already have observed that any payments made are entered to the Credit column, while receipts (money coming into the business) go into the Debit column. When the business pays a supplier, the amount is debited in the supplier account and credited in the bank account.

This example of double entry typifies how transactions are handled in accounts. As a rule, all asset accounts will be debited when assets are entering the business and credited when they are leaving the business. These accounts 'nominally' belong to the asset and not the business.

Tax Control Account

Another important Control Account is the **Tax Control Account**, which registers all the VAT receipts and payments. Figure 4.3 illustrates the end section of such a listing and was extracted from the Control Account History menu in the Nominal Ledger.

```
┌─────────────────────────────────────────────────────────────────────────┐
│ ┌───────────────────────────────────────────────────────────────────┐   │
│ │ Bookkeeper              Tax Control              26th July 199X     │   │
│ └───────────────────────────────────────────────────────────────────┘   │
│                                                                           │
│  A/C Ref. : 2200    Tax Code :  T   A/C Name : TAX CONTROL ACCOUNT        │
│                                                                           │
│  No.  Tp  Date    Ref       Details         Value      Debit     Credit   │
│                                                                           │
│   11  SC  30069X  300024  Scarves            0.88       0.88              │
│   12  SC  30069X  300027  Cricket starter set 2.98      2.98              │
│   15  PI  17079X  002091  Shirts and Shorts  61.25      61.25             │
│   16  PI  17079X  19291   Cricket sets       119.15    119.15             │
│   17  PI  17079X  800121  Basket Balls       36.75      36.75             │
│   18  PI  17079X  7118     Soccer Balls       56.00      56.00            │
│   20  PI  15079X  800102  Rugby Balls        35.00      35.00             │
│   21  PC  17079X          Soccer Balls Ret.   3.50                  3.50  │
│                                                                           │
│                                             Totals :   312.01     289.46  │
│                                             Balance :   22.55             │
│             Press  ESC  to finish,  RETURN  to continue                   │
└─────────────────────────────────────────────────────────────────────────┘
```

Fig 4.3

The Tax Control Account has been used to record all VAT payments and receipts that were passed through the Sales and Purchase Ledgers. When a customer is invoiced for goods sent, the Sales Account in the Nominal Ledger is credited by the nett amount. The VAT has then to be credited to the Tax Control Account to make up the total gross amount. This gross amount is then debited to the customer who is in receipt of the goods and now owes that amount to the business. Alternatively, when goods are purchased with VAT on them, the nominal account that records the purchase is debited by the nett amount, with the VAT being debited to the Tax Control Account.

The Tax Control Account shows, in transaction order, all VAT collected by the business on the credit side which has to be passed on to Customs & Excise. The VAT paid by the business is shown on the Debit side and can be claimed from Customs & Excise. If you observe the totals you will see that Figure 4.3 shows £289.46 has been collected while £312.01 has been paid out. If the firm were to settle the VAT with Customs & Excise, they would be able to claim the difference of £22.55. It is usually the case that businesses have to pay Customs & Excise.

Debtors Control Account

This can be examined through the **Control Account History** option of the Nominal Ledger. When a customer receives goods in advance of payment, you are already aware that a sales account in the Nominal Ledger is credited while the customer's account is debited. The Debtors Control Account is used within the Nominal Ledger system to record the totals of advances made to customers. The account shows, therefore, the total amount owing to the firm. This preserves the double entry system because, when a sale is made the sales account is credited while the Debtors' Control Account is debited.

When the customer makes a payment, the Debtors Control Account will be credited (so the debt outstanding is lowered), while the bank account is debited by the money being paid to the business.

The use of the Debtors Control Account means that all double entry transactions concerned with selling goods and services are confined only to the operation of the Nominal Ledger.

Creditors Control Account

This again can be examined through the **Control Account History** option of the Nominal Ledger. When a business receives goods from a supplier on account, the purchase account or some other asset account in the Nominal Ledger is debited while the supplier's account in the Purchase Ledger is credited. The Creditors Control Account is used within the Nominal Ledger system to record the totals of advances received from its suppliers. The account shows, therefore, the total amount owing by the business to its creditors. This also preserves the double entry system because, when credit purchases are made, an asset account is debited while the Creditors Control Account is credited.

When the firm makes a payment to its suppliers, the Creditors Control Account will be debited (so the debt outstanding is lowered) while the bank account is credited by the money being paid by the business.

The use of the Creditors Control Account means that all double entry transactions regarding purchases are confined to the operation of the Nominal Ledger.

Non-control accounts

The control accounts have been used by the Purchase and Sales Ledgers to summarise the transactions that have gone through. Later in this chapter, you will see how these control accounts are used further.

The Nominal Ledger holds many other accounts, some of which you have already used. In Figure 4.4 you will observe that nominal account 5001 was used to store all stock purchases.

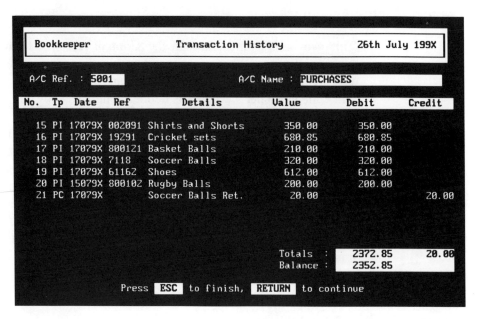

```
 Bookkeeper              Transaction History        26th July 199X

 A/C Ref. : 5001                    A/C Name : PURCHASES

 No.  Tp  Date    Ref        Details          Value       Debit      Credit

  15  PI 17079X 002091  Shirts and Shorts     350.00      350.00
  16  PI 17079X 19291   Cricket sets          680.85      680.85
  17  PI 17079X 800121  Basket Balls          210.00      210.00
  18  PI 17079X 7118    Soccer Balls          320.00      320.00
  19  PI 17079X 61162   Shoes                 612.00      612.00
  20  PI 15079X 800102  Rugby Balls           200.00      200.00
  21  PC 17079X         Soccer Balls Ret.      20.00                  20.00

                                     Totals :           2372.85       20.00
                                     Balance :          2352.85

              Press  ESC  to finish,  RETURN  to continue
```

Fig 4.4

Examination of nominal accounts can be done using the **Transaction History** option in the Nominal Ledger. The account in Figure 4.4 shows a number of debit entries which represent the purchases made from suppliers via the Purchase Ledger. Each one of these debit entries will have a corresponding credit entry in the Creditors Control Account. The single entry of £20.00 shown in the Credit column is a purchase Credit Note, which is entered as the opposite of the purchase invoices in the Debit column.

The trial balance

Figure 4.5 shows a trial balance, which can be accessed by selecting the **Trial Balance** option from the Nominal Ledger menu.

```
┌──────────────────────────────────────────────────────────────┐
│ Bookkeeper            Trial Balance            26th July 199X  │
└──────────────────────────────────────────────────────────────┘

        ┌──────┬────────────────────────┬──────────┬──────────┐
        │ Ref. │    Accounts Name        │  Debit   │  Credit  │
        └──────┴────────────────────────┴──────────┴──────────┘
         1001   STOCK                      2352.85
         1100   DEBTORS CONTROL ACCOUNT    1704.15
         1200   BANK CURRENT ACCOUNT                   1856.75
         2100   CREDITORS CONTROL ACCOUNT               388.75
         2200   TAX CONTROL ACCOUNT          22.55
         4000   SALES TYPE A                            638.09
         4001   SALES TYPE B                            465.87
         4002   SALES TYPE C                            508.09
         4009   DISCOUNTS ALLOWED                       222.00


                                         ┌──────────┬──────────┐
                                         │ 4079.55  │ 4079.55  │
                                         └──────────┴──────────┘
              Press  ESC  to finish,  RETURN  to continue
```

Fig 4.5

The significance of the figures is important as they represent, for each account, the nett balance. In the stock account, we can see that when all the debits and credits were taken into account, the debits exceeded the credits by £2352.85. The other accounts can be read in exactly the same way. You should observe from this that the bank account shows more has been spent than received.

When the figures in the debit and credit columns are added up they must be equal amounts. If each entry has been credited and debited in the Nominal Ledger, then all the debits must add up to all the credits and so must the nett differences shown in the trial balance.

NOMINAL LEDGER ORGANISATION

The Nominal Ledger function, as has already been seen, is very different from the Sales and Purchase Ledgers. It does, however, require a good deal of information from them. At this stage, it is worth examining how the Nominal Ledger function is structured with the aid of Figure 4.6.

The focal point in the Nominal Ledger function is the actual nominal accounts. Each nominal account has a name given to it which is determined by the business which uses the system. Account names will vary considerably, depending on the type of business using the system. Sage allows a default set-up which creates a series of accounts organised into a number of groups. If you have followed the guidelines set out in this book, you will have this set-up already with the defaults given by Sage. For most businesses, this set-up will probably suffice, perhaps with some alterations.

Given this layout, or any other, accounts have to be placed into a category.

These categories are important in order to extract various reports. The accounts are broken down into two main groups: Profit & Loss and Balance Sheet.

Profit & Loss

These include all accounts relating to transactions that contribute to making a profit. Such accounts fall into four sub-categories:

1 **Purchases** Accounts relating to buying stock. Such accounts will also include any goods returned to suppliers.

2 **Sales** Accounts relating to selling goods or services. Such accounts will also include any goods returned to the business by its customers.

3 **Direct expenses** These refer to the expenses directly linked with manufacturing of goods, e.g. factory wages, or the selling of goods, e.g. sales commission to sales staff.

4 **Overheads** These are expenses incurred generally in the running of the business, such as rent of property, electricity, administration, or car repairs.

Balance Sheet

These accounts also fall into four groupings:

1 **Financed by** Such accounts are used to hold transactions regarding the long-term financing of a business, such as share capital, long-term loans and accumulated retained profits.

2 **Current Liabilities** Such accounts refer to those debts owed by the business that will need repaying in the near future. An obvious example of this will be the sums owing to trade creditors as recorded in the Purchase Ledger. Another example would be any loans or overdrafts arranged over a short period of time.

3 **Fixed Assets** These accounts record transactions relating to the permanent assets of the business such as land, buildings, machinery, furniture, fixtures, fittings and motor vehicles. Also included with these accounts will be any depreciation on such assets which will come about as a result of wear and tear, obsolescence or, in the case of leaseholds, expiry date.

4 **Current Assets** These accounts hold transaction details regarding those assets of the business that will be required to be used in its operation, and so will be temporary in nature. Examples are stocks, trade debtors and money held in the bank.

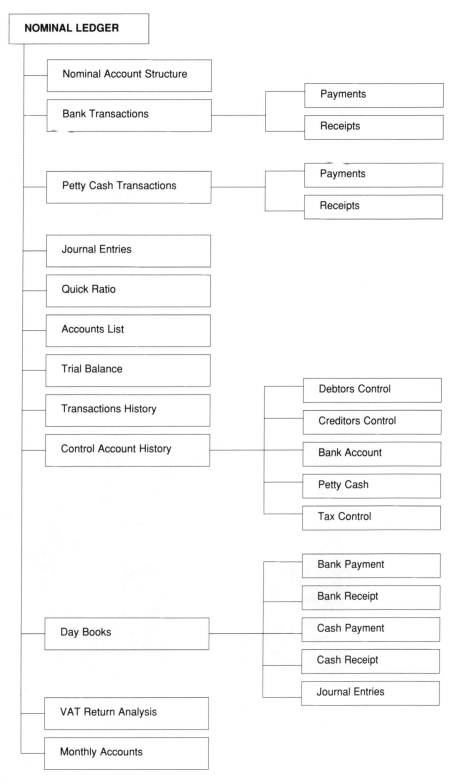

Fig 4.6

Most accounts will fall into their categories quite easily. Some accounts, however, will not fall so easily into a category at first and it will take experience to do this. In practice, an accountant will be involved in the process of setting up the structure of the Nominal Accounts system. If you are in any doubt about where an account should fall, then *ask*; do not attempt to guess.

Changing account details

From the Nominal Ledger menu, select **Nominal Account Structure** followed by **Account Name** and choose an existing account which you require to alter in some way. Figure 4.7 shows that account 5001 is being altered to TRADING PURCHASES. This may reflect more accurately what the account is being used for. In practice, a business will need an account that holds the opening value of stock when the accounts are first started and an account called purchases that will record the goods purchased over a trading period.

It is worth emphasising again that this account should be used for *trading* purchases only. Any purchases of goods for the running of the business, such as motor vehicles, must be posted to a fixed asset account.

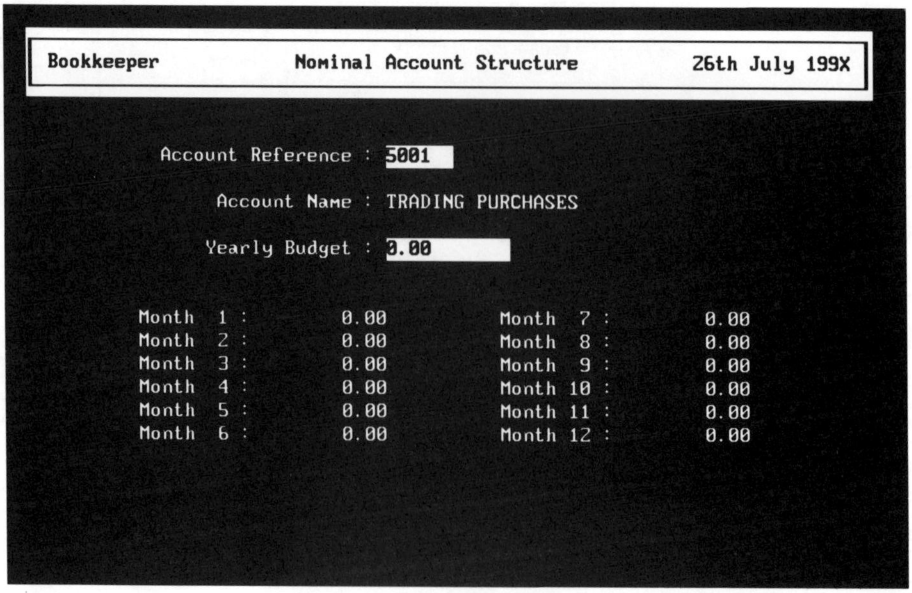

```
┌────────────────────────────────────────────────────────────────────┐
│ Bookkeeper          Nominal Account Structure        26th July 199X  │
└────────────────────────────────────────────────────────────────────┘



              Account Reference :  5001


               Account Name :  TRADING PURCHASES

               Yearly Budget :  0.00



     Month  1 :        0.00        Month  7 :        0.00
     Month  2 :        0.00        Month  8 :        0.00
     Month  3 :        0.00        Month  9 :        0.00
     Month  4 :        0.00        Month 10 :        0.00
     Month  5 :        0.00        Month 11 :        0.00
     Month  6 :        0.00        Month 12 :        0.00
```

Fig 4.7

Setting a budget

The Nominal Account structure screen also shows figures for budgets. The yearly budget allows you to enter a figure that you believe should not be exceeded over the year. There is little point in placing a budget figure for either trading purchases or sales, because you will aim to maximise sales in most cases, which will require a high amount of purchasing if sales demand proves to be high. A budget figure placed on these accounts will be used as a target figure rather than an attempt to keep within these limits.

When any alteration has been made, press **Esc** and ask the system to **Post** the changes. Figure 4.8 shows the effect of entering a budget on Advertising.

```
┌──────────────────────────────────────────────────────────────────────┐
│  Bookkeeper              Nominal Account Structure      26th July 199X │
└──────────────────────────────────────────────────────────────────────┘

            Account Reference :  5201

              Account Name  :  ADVERTISING

              Yearly Budget :      2400.00


        Month  1 : 200.00            Month  7 :      200.00
        Month  2 :      200.00       Month  8 :      200.00
        Month  3 :      200.00       Month  9 :      200.00
        Month  4 :      200.00       Month 10 :      200.00
        Month  5 :      200.00       Month 11 :      200.00
        Month  6 :      200.00       Month 12 :      200.00
```

Fig 4.8

When a yearly budget is entered, the system automatically spreads this evenly over 12 months. If this needs to be altered to vary monthly amounts, then you should go into each month and alter the figures accordingly. In the case of advertising, it may be the policy of the business to change its advertising plans over the year to reflect the possible seasonal variations in the sale of its products.

Budgets set in this instance are usually done in order to help control expenditure rather than set targets. Budgeting, for whatever reason, can help a business plan for its future and the presence of budget figures will also act as a useful indicator to the performance of the business.

Examining the Profit & Loss structure

From the Nominal Account structure you are able to alter the **Profit & Loss Format** to suit the business on a fairly flexible basis. In this option you are able to change the account format for Sales, Purchase, Direct Expenses and three Overhead categories. Figure 4.9 shows the category for Overheads (1).

Bookkeeper	Overheads (1)		26th July 199X

Category Heading	Low	High
SALARIES AND WAGES	7000	7099
RENT AND RATES	7100	7199
HEAT, LIGHT AND POWER	7200	7299
MOTOR EXPENSES	7300	7399
TRAVELLING AND ENTERTAINMENT	7400	7499
PRINTING AND STATIONERY	7500	7599
PROFESSIONAL FEES	7600	7699
EQUIPMENT HIRE AND RENTAL	7700	7799
MAINTENANCE	7800	7899
BANK CHARGES AND INTEREST	7900	7999
DEPRECIATION	8000	8099
BAD DEBTS	8100	8199
GENERAL EXPENSES	8200	8299
UNUSED CATEGORY		
UNUSED CATEGORY		

Fig 4.9

The line Salaries and wages shows that all these accounts are numbered between 7000 and 7099. This method of grouping accounts will prove useful when extracting final accounts and also serves as a good way of helping users find their way around an accounting system. The system allows an operator to alter the format and should be so laid out that, if new accounts are needed, there is room within a category to add these.

At this stage it is well worth exploring the other formats from the Nominal Ledger structure before moving on.

CASH AND BANK TRANSACTION

In this next stage you will examine further how cash and bank transactions are processed in the accounts. When you made a payment to a supplier through the Purchase Ledger, the bank account in the Nominal Ledger was credited by the payment amount, while the creditors' control account was debited. We must now examine the effect of paying, for example, an electricity bill.

Paying expenses

When paying an expense, the bank account will, as before, be credited by the payment. In the case of the electricity bill, the electricity account has to be debited by the payment. Consequently, the double entry has been made for us. Figure 4.10 shows a series of bank payments made via a batch entry form which is done through **Bank Transactions, Payments** from the Nominal Ledger menu.

```
┌──────────────────────────────────────────────────────────────────────┐
│  Bookkeeper              Bank Payments            27th July 199X       │
│                                                                        │
│  N/C Bank : BANK CURRENT ACCOUNT           Tax Rate :      0.000       │
│  N/C Name :                                Batch Total :  2929.50      │
│                                                                        │
│   N/C  Dep. Date  Cheque      Details      Nett Amnt Tc Tax Amnt       │
│                                                                        │
│   7200  0 27079X 092921 Wessex Electric plc  176.00 T1    12.50        │
│   7003  0 27079X 092922 Jane Blake           450.00 T9     0.00        │
│   7100  0 27079X 092923 Property Services    300.00 T9     0.00        │
│   7104  0 27079X 092923 Building Insurance   750.00 T0     0.00        │
│   7006  0 28079X 092925 Inland Revenue       180.00 T0     0.00        │
│   7102  0 27079X 092926 Wessex Water         233.00 T0     0.00        │
│   7303  0 27079X 092927 T K Hott Ins. Brok.  321.00 T9     0.00        │
│   7502  0 27079X 092928 BT                   192.00 T1    25.00        │
│   7903  0 27079X 092930 ICCB Loan Interest   290.00 T9     0.00        │
│                                                                        │
│                                            2892.00        37.50        │
└──────────────────────────────────────────────────────────────────────┘
```

Fig 4.10

In each case the bank account is credited and a respective overhead account is debited. When entering the details, you are required to enter the Nominal Code in the **N/C** column. If you know that the account starts with **7**, then entering this first character and pressing **Enter** (Return) will cause all the accounts prefixed with 7 to be displayed. You need only highlight the account to debit and press **Enter** (Return). The details column can be used for stating exactly what appears on the cheque.

When you have entered all the account details into the computer, the figures are individually posted to the accounts for future inspection. It is still wise for a business to keep copies of all cheque counterfoils for future reference.

Paying for non-expenses

When a cheque is used to purchase assets the effect on the accounts will be exactly the same as for other purchases, as the bank account is credited and another account debited.

Figure 4.11 is an entry form showing payments for non-expense items. Such payments will result in the bank balance lowering with some other asset balance rising. In the first line, the business has paid for a 10-year lease. This gives the business an asset worth £100 000 but lowers the bank balance by that amount. Likewise, the office equipment is worth a total of £7500 more and the business owns a car worth £3000, all at the cost of the bank balance.

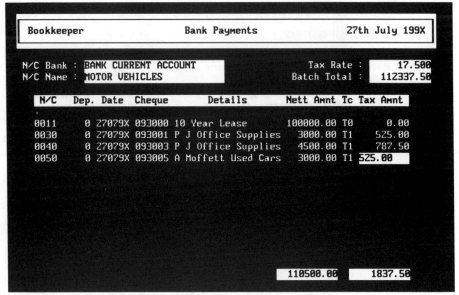

```
┌─────────────────────────────────────────────────────────────────────────┐
│  Bookkeeper              Bank Payments            27th July 199X          │
└─────────────────────────────────────────────────────────────────────────┘

  N/C Bank : BANK CURRENT ACCOUNT          Tax Rate :      17.500
  N/C Name : MOTOR VEHICLES                Batch Total :  112337.50

    ┌──────────────────────────────────────────────────────────────────┐
    │  N/C   Dep. Date  Cheque      Details      Nett Amnt Tc Tax Amnt   │
    └──────────────────────────────────────────────────────────────────┘
      0011    0 27079X 093000 10 Year Lease     100000.00 T0       0.00
      0030    0 27079X 093001 P J Office Supplies  3000.00 T1     525.00
      0040    0 27079X 093003 P J Office Supplies  4500.00 T1     787.50
      0050    0 27079X 093005 A Moffett Used Cars  3000.00 T1     525.00

                                          ┌───────────┐  ┌──────────┐
                                          │ 110500.00 │  │ 1837.50  │
                                          └───────────┘  └──────────┘
```

Fig 4.11

The effect of paying for expenses will be to reduce the amount of profit the business will make, as all such costs are 'sunk' in that they cannot be recovered. For example, when an electricity bill has been paid, it is for electricity consumed and has left no value remaining to the business. When an asset is purchased such as stock or motor vehicles, the business holds on to something with a value and cannot be regarded as contributing to costs. If an asset is sold for more than it cost to purchase, then it is only at this stage that it contributes directly to the profit of the business.

You should also note that the purchasing of either stock for resale or assets will be made through the Purchase Ledger if they are being purchased on a credit basis. It is possible, however, to bypass the need for the Purchase Ledger if nominal accounts are set up for creditors.

Bank receipts

When cheques are received from customers for payment of goods invoiced, these will need to go through the Sales Ledger so that they are off-set against customers' accounts. Other receipts by cheque will go through this system in the Nominal Ledger.

All bank receipts will have the effect of debiting the bank account and crediting some other account. In Figure 4.12 some receipts have been entered. The top two receipts are from the owners of the business and have been used to credit their personal Share Capital accounts. The third receipt has been used to credit a revenue account.

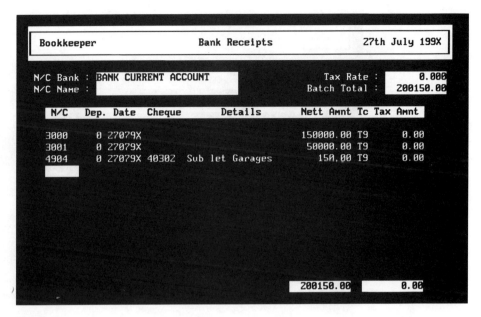

Fig 4.12

A revenue account has the opposite effect on profits to an expense account in that it will cause profits to rise. For many non-trading companies, such as solicitors or estate agents, their profits will depend largely on revenues received in return for professional services.

Many receipts will have the effect of raising the amount of finance to the business. In the case of share capital, money is received from shareholders and placed into the bank account. This has raised both the assets of the business and the 'financed by' accounts of the business, which are the shareholders' funds.

PETTY CASH TRANSACTIONS

A business will always need to handle some cash. For a retail business, this is likely to be a quite considerable sum, as most of their sales will probably be for cash.

To begin with, you ought to start the business off with some cash in its 'float'. To do this, you will need to remove some money from the bank (credit the bank account) and place it into the cash account (debit petty cash). To do this you will need to make a Journal entry. From the main Nominal Ledger menu select **Journal Entry**. You will see that you are immediately asked for a Nominal Account reference. Select the Bank Account number and, using Figure 4.13 to guide you, credit the Bank Account by £500. After this, debit the Petty Cash Account by £500.

```
┌─────────────────────────────────────────────────────────────────┐
│ ┌───────────────────────────────────────────────────────────┐   │
│ │  Bookkeeper            Journal Entries        27th July 199X│   │
│ └───────────────────────────────────────────────────────────┘   │
│                                                                   │
│      Date : 270791                      Reference : A100          │
│   N/C Name :                            Batch Total :      0.00   │
│                                                                   │
│         N/C   Dep.    Details       Tc   Debit     Credit         │
│                                                                   │
│        1200    0 Transfer to Cash   T9             500.00         │
│        1230    0 From Bank          T9   500.00                   │
│                                                                   │
│                                                                   │
│                                                                   │
│                                                                   │
│            Batch Total  MUST  be  ZERO  before exit               │
└─────────────────────────────────────────────────────────────────┘
```

Fig 4.13

Using Journal entries in this way is about the only time you will need to identify which account has to be debited and credited.

Once this has been posted, you will now have sufficient cash available to make some cash payments. From the main Nominal Ledger menu **Petty Cash Transactions** operates in almost the identical way to bank payments. Figure 4.14 gives an example of a batch of cash payments, all of which reduce the amount of cash.

```
┌─────────────────────────────────────────────────────────────────┐
│ ┌───────────────────────────────────────────────────────────┐   │
│ │  Bookkeeper            Cash Payments          27th July 199X│   │
│ └───────────────────────────────────────────────────────────┘   │
│                                                                   │
│                                         Tax Rate :      17.500    │
│   N/C Name :                            Batch Total :   128.81    │
│                                                                   │
│     N/C   Dep. Date   Ref.     Details    Nett Amnt Tc Tax Amnt   │
│                                                                   │
│    7400   0 27079X C00201 Train Fare        13.62 T1    2.38      │
│    7501   0 27079X C00202 Postage           54.00 T1    9.45      │
│    7504   0 27079X C00203 Paper Supplies    23.00 T1    4.03      │
│    7500   0 27079X C00205 Photocopier Toner 19.00 T1    3.33      │
│                                                                   │
│                                                                   │
│                                            109.62        19.19    │
└─────────────────────────────────────────────────────────────────┘
```

Fig 4.14

Entering cash receipts works in exactly the same way. Such receipts are normally from cash sales and it is worth your while entering a couple of such transactions. When dealing with cash, a situation cannot arise where more cash leaves an account than enters it. If the petty cash shows a credit balance on the trial balance it would imply a negative holding of cash, which does not make sense. With respect to the Bank Statement, a credit balance which appeared in the Trial Balance on Figure 4.5 would show that the business has an overdraft with the bank.

Figure 4.15 demonstrates a further example of money being transferred from the Bank Current Account to a Deposit Account.

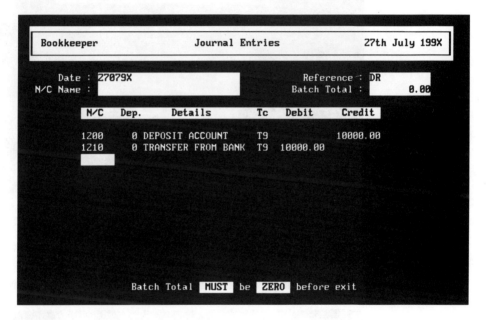

Fig 4.15

LIQUIDITY

For most businesses it is important to keep a close eye on their liquidity. This involves looking at the liquid assets of the business such as money in the bank or petty cash and comparing these with any outstanding debts owing by the business that fall due fairly soon.

The exact definition of a liquid asset is open to some interpretation by businesses. Basically, any asset that is cash or can be turned into cash within a short period (say six weeks) can be regarded as a liquid asset. Because such liquidity is open to interpretation, Sage allows you to define for yourself what assets are liquid.

From the Nominal Ledger select **Quick Ratio** and then **Edit** to allow you to decide first what you regard as liquid assets. At this stage, you would work through all the asset accounts deciding which are liquid. In addition to this, you will need to work through all the accounts deciding on what the current liabilities are. Figure 4.16 gives an example of such accounts.

Escaping from this menu and choosing to **view** the quick ratio will give something similar to the trial balance. Each account selected in the editing of quick ratios is listed with the balance shown as either debit or credit.

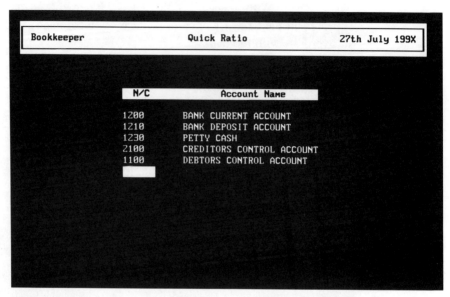

Fig 4.16

From Figure 4.17 you will observe that the debit figures exceed the credit figures by £84 618.22 which is a very high figure. If the figure was reversed so that the credits were greater than the debits, it would imply that the business is likely to have difficulty meeting its financial commitments.

Bookkeeper	Quick Ratio		27th July 199X

N/C	Account Name	Debit	Credit
1200	BANK CURRENT ACCOUNT	72526.25	
1210	BANK DEPOSIT ACCOUNT	10000.00	
1230	PETTY CASH	776.57	
2100	CREDITORS CONTROL ACCOUNT		388.75
1100	DEBTORS CONTROL ACCOUNT	1704.15	

84618.22

Press **ESC** to finish, **RETURN** to continue

Fig 4.17

DOUBLE ENTRY SUMMARISED

Throughout this chapter, you have been made aware of the principle of double entry. An understanding of this is important to be able to get the best out of the reports available and to be able to correct any errors. It is also needed if you are to make effective use of the Journal Entry option.

Figure 4.18 shows further examples of how Journal Entries are used to make double entries to the nominal accounts.

Bookkeeper				Journal Entries			27th July 199X	

No.	Tp	A/C	N/C	Date	Ref.	Details	Debit	Credit
48	JC		1200	27079X	a100	Transfer to Cash		500.00
49	JD		1230	27079X	a100	From Bank	500.00	
55	JC		1200	27079X	DR	DEPOSIT ACCOUNT		10000.00
56	JD		1210	27079X	DR	TRANSFER FROM BANK	10000.00	
57	JC		0021	30079X	DR	Plant Depreciation		500.00
58	JD		8000	30079X	DR	Plant & Machinery	500.00	
59	JC		0030	30079X	DR	Computer Dep.		400.00
60	JD		8000	30079X	DR	Computer	500.00	
61	JC		0030	30079X	DR	Typewriters		100.00
							11500.00	11500.00

Press **ESC** to finish, **RETURN** to continue

Fig 4.18

The first two entries were used to transfer money from the bank current account into the petty cash account with the next two entries moving money from the bank current account to a deposit account. The other entries were made to depreciate assets. The effect of depreciation is to create a valuation of fixed assets below the value paid for them. This is an attempt to give a true current value to the assets of the business. To do this you will have to credit accounts especially set up for the depreciation of the assets in question. You could, however, credit the actual asset account. The account that has to be debited will be an expense account called Depreciation.

The journal is used to enter all Nominal Ledger entries that cannot be carried out through the Purchase and Sales Ledger or with bank and cash transactions in the Nominal Ledger.

To use the journal entry effectively, you have to be clear about when to debit or credit an account. The following rules may help you in future:

1 Fixed Asset Accounts

Debit These accounts are debited when more of the asset is being acquired. As the debit items increase, so the value of fixed assets, before depreciation, increase.

Credit When an asset is disposed of the account is credited. If an account is set up to show provision for depreciation, then this account is credited each time an asset is depreciated.

2 Trading Accounts

Debit Represents goods being received by the business. This can take the form of purchases of stock or goods returned from customers.

Credit Represents goods leaving the business. Sales of goods to customers and goods returned to suppliers will appear on the credit side of these accounts.

3 Current Assets

Debit Represents assets being received by the business. When the bank or cash accounts show debit entries, you know money has been received. The Debtors Control Account debit entries show that customers' debt has risen.

Credit Represents assets leaving the firm. When the bank or cash accounts show credit entries, you know payments have been made. The Creditors Control Account credit entries show that the amount owing to suppliers has risen.

4 Expenses

Debit Represents a payment being made for an expense.

Credit Represents a refund being received on the account.

5 Revenue

Debit Represents a refund being paid by the business.

Credit Money being received for a service such as income from property, interest on investments, fees paid by clients and so on.

6 Current Liabilities

Debit Here liabilities are being reduced, for example by payment to a supplier or the clearing of a bank overdraft.

Credit This increases money owing by the business such as a credit purchase from a supplier.

7 Financed by

Debit This reduces the money being used to finance the business, for example by a withdrawal of money by an owner or shareholder of the business.

Credit This increases the finance to the business, for example the raising of more share capital or a long-term loan from a bank.

Throughout the last three chapters you have probably been entering figures in a manner that would not be suitable for a business starting off with the Sage package for the first time. To get an appreciation of how a business might make a start with the package, you will be given the chance to examine three case studies in Chapter 10.

THE FINANCIAL YEAR

Each business will, for tax and accounting purposes, have a financial year. The start of a financial year will depend on when the business was formed but will normally be the first day of a month and run for 12 months. At the end of the year there are many important activities that have to be carried out.

At the end of the year, the business must draw up a statement of Profit & Loss. This can be carried out for you by Sage if your accounts are correctly structured. Before doing this, the business ought to carry out the following tasks:

1   Finish posting all transactions for the year. This can occupy a good deal of an operator's time in trying to chase up invoices and receipts that have not yet been entered to the system.

2   Backup on to a floppy disk *all* data files for the year, being careful to label your disk as data files as at END OF YEAR with a date. The need for backing up cannot be over-emphasised. Once a computer system has been running for some time, it is often the case that the data generated is worth more in value than the entire computer system. Once data is properly backed up, there should be no possibility of a disaster in terms of data processing.

3   Print an **Aged Debtors Report** and check the Outstanding Debtors total against the nominal ledger **Debtors Control Account**.

4   Print statements of account or Sales Ledger transaction histories so that customers can be notified of the state of their accounts.

5 Extract all required Purchase Ledger listings.

6 Print out Transaction Histories for all the accounts in the Profit & Loss section. When the new year is started, all Profit & Loss accounts will be cleared of their transactions.

7 Extract an audit trail to give a complete set for the year.

8 Print any analysis reports and the **Tax Control** listing.

9 Run **Year End** routine from the **Utilities** part of the main menu.

10 Backup data files again, being careful to label your disk as data files as at BEGINNING OF YEAR.

If backing up has been done properly *at both stages* and it is found that a mistake or omission has been made, then you will always be able to restore the backup and start the end-of-year process.

Running the year end program

When this program is run you are warned about the consequences of your action with the message:

'This routine will post Journal Debits and Journal Credits, as appropriate, to all Nominal Ledger Accounts appearing in the Profit & Loss Report to zero the balances in all these accounts. A final balancing Journal entry will be posted to the Retained Profit & Loss Account.'

When you press **Enter** (Return) to confirm your action, a statement is shown of Profit & Loss in the form given in Figure 4.19.

Each account in the Profit & Loss accounts is listed with the amount that was either credited or debited, to leave it with a zero balance. The debits and credits columns are added up with the balance figure (the difference between the totals) to be posted to the Profit and Loss Account. In Figure 4.19 you will observe that the business shows a profit of £4045.42.

Start of the next year

The accounts will now be ready for the start of the new year with the following state of affairs:

1 All Profit & Loss Accounts will have no entries in them.

2 The remaining Balance Sheet accounts will have a single figure of balance carried down from the previous year.

N/C	Account Name	Debit	Credit
4000	SALES TYPE A	983.09	
4001	SALES TYPE B	465.87	
4002	SALES TYPE C	508.09	
4009	DISCOUNTS ALLOWED	222.00	
4904	RENT INCOME	150.00	
5001	TRADING PURCHASES		2372.85
7003	STAFF SALARIES		450.00
7006	EMPLOYERS N.I.		180.00
7100	RENT		300.00
7102	WATER RATES		233.00
7104	PREMISES INSURANCE		750.00
7200	ELECTRICITY		176.00
7303	VEHICLE INSURANCE		321.00
7400	TRAVELLING		13.62
7500	PRINTING		19.00
7501	POSTAGE AND CARRIAGE		54.00
7502	TELEPHONE		192.00
7504	OFFICE STATIONERY		23.00
7903	LOAN INTEREST PAID		290.00
8000	DEPRECIATION		1000.00
3200	PROFIT AND LOSS ACCOUNT	4045.42	

Fig 4.19

3   The Profit & Loss Account will hold the profit made.

If you have any stock left over, then the value of this stock should be added to the profit of the business. The reason for this is that, in the example given in this chapter, we have assumed all the stock purchased has been sold. To correct this you could start the year off by valuing your stock and debiting the Opening Stock account with this amount and then crediting Profit & Loss Account by this amount.

If the business is to distribute the retained profit for paying tax or giving to shareholders, then it will need to do so by crediting the bank account that pays out the money and debiting the Profit & Loss Account of the business.

Conclusion and Exercises

As a way of gaining a greater knowledge of the Nominal Ledger, try the following questions. If you have already set up the Nominal Ledger as you worked through this chapter, then some of the tasks should be missed out.

1   Extract an Accounts List in order to determine where your control accounts are.

2   a   Determine the grouping of accounts being used for the Fixed Assets and Current Assets.
   b   Create the following Fixed Asset accounts:
      Fixtures and fittings

Land and buildings (property)
Motor vehicle
Office machinery

c Create the following Current Asset accounts:
Bank deposit
Opening stock

3 **a** Determine the groupings of accounts being used for Expenses and Revenue.

b Create the following Expense accounts, placing a budget figure of your choice where applicable:

Account	Budget
Carriage and postage	Yes
Corporation tax	No
Depreciation	No
Electricity	No
Entertainment	Yes
Insurance	Yes
Printing and stationery	Yes
Rent on garages	Yes
Telephone	Yes
Travel expenses	Yes
Wages and salaries	Yes
Water rates	Yes

c Create the following Revenue accounts:
Client consultancy receipts
Interest received on bank deposit account

4 Create the following Financed By accounts:
Shareholders equity
Long-term bank loan

5 Enter an opening trial balance giving figures for at least the following accounts:

Bank deposit
Customer receipts
Electricity
Fixtures and fittings
Land and buildings (property)
Long-term bank loan
Motor vehicle
Office machinery
Opening stock
Printing and stationery
Shareholders equity

6 Now enter some cash transactions and bank transactions for the following:

   a *Payments*
   A motor vehicle
   An electricity bill
   Wages
   Insurance premiums
   Telephone bill
   b *Receipts*
   Client consultancy fees
   Interest on bank deposit
   Cash sales
   Refund of insurance premiums

7 Now make Journal entries for the following transaction types:

   Transfer some money into Petty Cash
   Depreciation of motor vehicles

8 Determine whether any VAT is owing and settle the account with a cheque. If you are due to receive VAT from HM Customs and Excise, then you should enter a receipt against the VAT account.

9 Select a number of expense accounts as a way of transferring cash from Petty Cash. If you are left with any balance in Petty Cash, then transfer this money to your Bank Account.

10 Extract the following reports as a way of examining the effects of the tasks undertaken:

   A trial balance
   Control Account Histories for all Control accounts
   History of transactions on the non-control accounts
   Quick Ratio

5 Advanced ledger work

INTRODUCTION

This chapter takes you through a number of important features required in most businesses. The work on the ledgers in this chapter is not available to Sage Bookkeeper but only available to **Accountant, Accountant Plus** and **Financial Controller**.

In the last chapter, you dealt with ending a year of trading and clearing out many Balance Sheet accounts, leaving only balances brought down from the previous year in the new accounts and opening completely fresh Profit & Loss Accounts. You will need to address the problem of accounts becoming too large as the year progresses and find a way of streamlining the accounts so that they are manageable while not losing their completeness and accuracy.

This chapter will start by examining some of the more advanced features of managing the ledgers more effectively. One of the more important uses of a computer is to be able to manage accounts efficiently and effectively especially when they become large in number.

An important requirement later in this chapter will be to make alterations to your accounts in the Nominal Ledger so that the final accounts produced at the end of any year truly reflect the performance of the business. This was touched upon in Chapter 4 when you accounted for depreciation on fixed assets. This chapter will take this a stage further as well as showing how to adjust expenses and revenues to reflect the true overheads and income of the business in a trading period.

MANAGING THE SALES LEDGER

Opening balances

When a business starts a Sales Ledger for the first time, it must set up all its customer accounts *and* enter their opening balances before the Sales Ledger can be used on a day-to-day basis.

The principle is quite straightforward. First you enter the customer details for all customers who owe the business money. Secondly, determine how much each customer owes. From the Batched Data Entry you should then choose to enter a Sales Invoice. At this point, you can enter all individual invoice details that are still outstanding as though the invoices had just been raised. Alternatively, you can enter a single outstanding value. If you choose the latter, then you will enter the following transactions data:

1   The Nominal Account code must be the code for the SUSPENSE ACCOUNT which Sage sets up as 0100

2   *Inv* entry should be **O/Bal**

3   *Details* entry should be **Opening Balance**

The effect of this is to debit the Debtors Control Account by the amount owing and, if you used the single opening balance method, credit the Suspense Account by this amount. Later in this chapter you will examine the role of the suspense account and what you have to do about the transactions in it.

Returned cheques

This refers to the event of a cheque that has been received by a customer being returned by the bank after it has been deposited. When the cheque was first received, you will have debited the bank account and credited the debtors control account in the Nominal Ledger, and credited the customer account in the Sales Ledger. When the cheque has been returned by the bank, you will need to get the computer to reverse this process completely.

Sage allows you to do this automatically with its Sales Ledger option **Refunds**. From the Sales Ledger menu select **Refunds** and you are given two more options. For handling returned cheques, select the option **Cancel Cheque**. You will now be asked to select the Sales Ledger account which has to register the returned cheque. Figure 5.1 shows an example of a customer whose cheque has been returned (bounced) by the bank.

If there are many transaction lines, you should use the arrow keys to move between these lines and press the **Enter** (Return) key to select the cheque to cancel. The computer will then enter into the STATUS heading the word BOUNCED. You will then need to press the **Esc** key to Abandon, Edit or Post the transaction details.

When the activity is complete and the cheque is recorded as bounced and posted as such, the transaction posting will be made as required.

Cancelling invoices

You may need to cancel an invoice previously entered. Such a need can arise when a replacement invoice has to be raised because there are a large number of errors in the original one. In this instance, it is best to cancel an invoice previously entered and generate a new one. Alternatively, an invoice may have

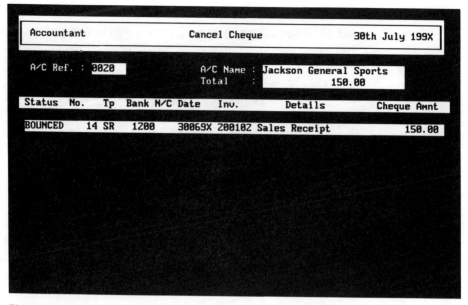

Accountant			Cancel Cheque				30th July 199X

A/C Ref. : **0020**

A/C Name : **Jackson General Sports**
Total   : **150.00**

Status	No.	Tp	Bank N/C	Date	Inv.	Details	Cheque Amnt
BOUNCED	14	SR	1200	30069X	200102	Sales Receipt	150.00

Fig 5.1

been sent in error to the wrong customer and you need to cancel an invoice on one customer and then generate a new invoice for another customer.

For whatever reason, the effect is similar to processing a cheque that has been returned. On the Nominal Ledger you will need to credit the Debtors Control Account (reduce what is owing) by the complete invoice amount and debit all the Nominal sales accounts that were previously credited (lower the sales value). On the Sales Ledger, you will need to credit the customer account as though the invoice had been settled.

As with returned cheques, Sage allows you to do this automatically with its Sales Ledger option Refunds. From the Sales Ledger menu select **Refunds** and you are given two more options. For cancelling invoices, select the option **Cancel Invoice**. You will now be asked to select the Sales Ledger account which stores the invoice, and then select the invoice to be cancelled in the same way as you cancelled a cheque.

Contra entries

The situation often arises when a business deals with another business as both a supplier and a customer. In other words, a business sells to another business and buys from it. In this instance an arrangement may be made where, instead of paying for all your supplies from this business and then invoicing it for all that is owing, you simply settle the difference between you. Entering a transaction that cancels an amount owing by you with an amount owing to you is called a **contra entry**. Before you attempt this, it is important to understand the stages involved.

Let us suppose that a business is both a customer and a supplier. The amount supplied by this business has been invoiced at £345 which is now outstanding. You have also supplied goods to this business as a customer and have invoiced it for £290 which is also outstanding. Some simple arithmetic will tell you that the difference between you is £55 in favour of the other business. To make a contra entry, you would firstly pay the £55 to the business as a supplier in the normal way through Sage Purchase Ledger as a payment, to leave the balances the same. Secondly, through the Sales Ledger, you choose Contra Entry to settle the amounts. The result, therefore, is first to credit the Bank Account by £55 and debit the Creditors Control Account by this amount in the Nominal Ledger. On the Purchase Ledger, the account has been debited by £55.

The effect of a contra entry on the nominal entry was to credit the Debtors Control Account by £290, so reducing the amount owing to it, and debit the Creditors Control Account by £290, so reducing what the firm owes to its suppliers. For a contra entry to work, the business will need to exist in both Sales Ledger and Purchase Ledger. A contra entry in this case will have credited a Sales Ledger account and debited a Purchase Ledger account.

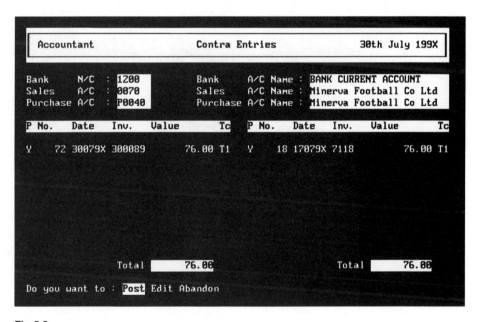

Fig 5.2

Figure 5.2 shows an example of a contra entry. Before you can start, you will have to ensure similar accounts exist in both the Sales and Purchase Ledgers. In the example shown here, Minerva Football Co Ltd, which existed in the Sales Ledger, has been created in the Purchase Ledger. Create such an account now and generate a purchase invoice so that you have debt outstanding with which to process a contra entry. Also, ensure you have at least one sales invoice outstanding.

The set-up from screen in Fig 5.2 shows Minerva Football Co Ltd as a Sales Ledger Account 0070 and Purchase Ledger Account P0040. The state of affairs before selecting Contra Entries was:

Sales invoice outstanding	£105.75
Purchase invoice outstanding	£76.00
Net amount owing to us	£29.75

If your figures are different, then adjust them so that you know what the difference is. Also note that, in comparison to the earlier example, it is our business which is now owed more than we owe and not the other way around. The steps involved are:

1   From the Sales Ledger enter a receipt of £29.75 to settle the difference. If the balance was in favour of Minerva, then we would do this via the Purchase Ledger instead.

2   Now select **Contra Entries** from the Sales Ledger menu.

3   Select the **Bank Nominal Account** that will be used to record the contra payment and receipt. The nett effect on the bank account will be zero, but a record needs to be kept.

4   Select both the Sales and Purchase Account references.

5   Now you need to work through a list of invoices on both the Purchase and Sales Ledgers selecting for both which invoices are to be settled. In the case of accounts shown in Figure 5.2 there is only one invoice on each side. The total columns below must equal each other before a posting can be made. For this reason, it is important to record the payment made first so that a balanced total is possible. Using the up, down, left and right arrow keys you can move to the invoices you require, using the Enter (Return) key to select the ones to settle. 'Y' appears in the Paid Column (P) to indicate those chosen.

6   When the selections have been made and the totals are equal, press the **Esc** key to finish and decide whether to Post, Edit or Abandon. If the balances are not equal, you will not be allowed to post the transaction.

The overall effect of this transaction on the Nominal Ledger has been to reduce both the creditors (amount owed to others) and debtors (amount owed to us). Also, the receipt from Minerva had the effect of raising the amount of money in the bank. If this were a Journal entry then the result would have been:

	Dr	Cr
Debtors Control Account		105.75
Creditors Control Account	76.00	
Bank Account	29.75	
Totals	105.75	105.75

Bad debts

The structure within Sage Sales Ledger for this option is shown in Figure 5.3.

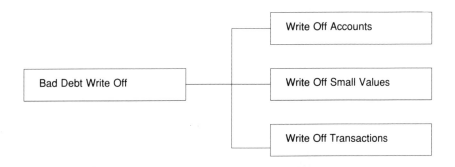

Fig 5.3

A bad debt occurs when your business decides no longer to pursue money owing and shows in its accounts that this debt is no longer regarded as an asset to the business. As shown in Figure 5.3, there are three ways of recording bad debts.

1   Firstly, you can write off an entire account as a bad debt. This would occur if a customer is regarded as not worth pursuing as a debtor or becomes bankrupt. In this instance the account is credited with the amount of bad debt (we pay the bill). The effect on the Nominal Ledger is to credit the Debtors Control Account and debit an account called Bad Debt, which is an expense account and so reduces profit. If a major customer is written off who owes a good deal of money, then this can be devastating on the profits of a business. To write off an account, select the **Write Off Accounts** option through the menu structure and then select the account.

2   The second kind of bad debt write off is when a business decides to write off all small sums owing. If, for example you decide to write off all outstanding debts of customers valued at less than £1.50 because it would be too costly to chase, then Sage has the provision for doing this. Each account with such a sum owing would be credited by the amounts written off. The effect on the Nominal Ledger would be to credit the Debtors

Control Account by the total and debit the Bad Debt Account by the same amount. In the longer term it may keep down the cost of debt recovery, such as posting letters requesting the money, sending statements of account, and the various administrative charges. To write off small values, select the **Write Off Small Values** option through the menu structure. You will now be asked for a value. The value entered cannot exceed £100, as this is not regarded as a small value. The system will guide you through each such transaction, asking whether you want this amount written off.

3   The third method is write off a transaction. For this you would need an audit trail which lists all the transactions and gives a required transactions number. To write off a transaction select the **Write Off Transactions** option through the menu structure and then select the transaction number.

Mailing customers

There are going to be many occasions when a business wishes to mail all of its customers. This section will examine the way in which Sage allows you to send personalised letters to all customers or a selected range of customers. In the first example, you will see how you can send a letter to all those customers who have debts outstanding for more than 30 days. It may also be useful to send customers some promotions literature which has been especially written to suit a given circumstance.

The principle of the mailing offered by Sage is that each customer receives the same letter but with altered details that apply to them only – such as their name, credit limit or amount of debt outstanding. To see how it works, select **Letters** from the Sales Ledger menu. You will first be asked if the letters are to go to customers who have exceeded their credit limit. If you answer **Y**(es), then only those customers who have exceeded their credit limit will receive a letter. However, you should be aware that, even if a credit limit has not been exceeded, customers should still make payments within a reasonable time after an invoice has been sent.

The next question asks if you want to send letters to those customers with a zero balance. If you answer **Y**(es) then customers who owe you nothing will receive a letter, something you might want if you are sending out promotional literature.

The third question asks for a number relating to the number of days the debt has been outstanding. You can answer 0, 30, 60, 90 or 120. If (say) you answer 30, then all those customers with debt outstanding for more than 30 days will receive a letter.

Lower and Upper Account reference allows you to select a range of customers to whom you want to send letters. If you want to send letters to all of them, simply accept the default values offered by pressing **Enter** (Return) on both. The date of the report may be important to change if your particular letter uses it. The file name is the name of the file that holds the details of the letter. The final question asks if output is to go to the printer or to a file for later printing.

Figure 5.4 is an example of a letter sent using the following selections:

Credit Limit Exceeded	N
Zero Balances	N
No of Days outstanding	30
Lower Account Reference	00000000
Upper Account Reference	ZZZZZZZZ
Date of Report	[system date]
Input File name	overdue. let
Printer or File	P

Jackson General Sports   25 September 199–
100 High Street
Glasgow
GL1 5HG

Dear Sirs

OVERDUE ACCOUNT £   329.00

We refer to the above balance which is still outstanding on your account. May we remind you that our terms are strictly 30 days nett and £   179.00 is more than 60 days overdue.

Your remittance by return would be appreciated.

Yours faithfully
SAGESOFT LTD

Paul Walker
COMPANY ACCOUNTANT

Fig 5.4

The details in the letter will probably not match those required for your particular business. You will need, therefore, to alter the details to match, or create a new letter.

Go to the main Sage menu and select **Utilities**. From here choose **Stationery Layouts** followed by **Accounts Letters**. The computer will now ask you to enter the name of the file that stores the letter. Figure 5.5 shows the original file called OVERDUE.LET which was used to send the letters to customers in the earlier example (Fig 5.4). The screen also shows that the name of the company accountant has been changed.

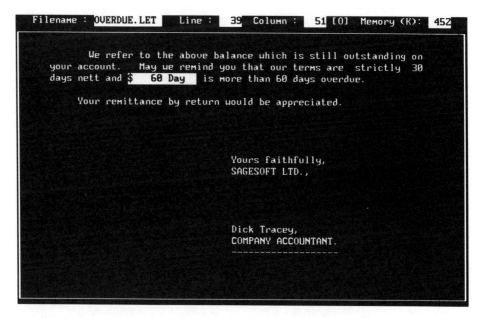

Fig 5.5

After the computer has found and loaded the file, use the arrow keys to move around the letter. If you want to delete any text, then use the **Delete** or **Del** key to do it. Text can be inserted by typing in what you want. It is well worth spending time practising this now, as you will come across it again on a number of occasions in this book.

When you have made the necessary changes, press the **Esc** key. Saving the changes will have the effect of making the changes permanent. If you feel you have made too many errors, then you can always choose the Abandon option and start again.

You can examine the changes by returning to the Sales Ledger and printing the letter again.

Next you should attempt to print a letter of your own. Returning to the **Utilities** menu, select **Stationery Layouts** followed by **Accounts Letters**. Instead of accepting the filename suggested, enter your own. The letter shown in Figure 5.6 was called **promote.let** and was created to inform customers of their credit limits and inform them about cash discounts for prompt payments. When you select the filename, the computer will indicate that it is to create a new file and the screen will be blank inside the edit box.

The text highlighted with a dark background indicates the positioning of field data extracted from the data in the Sales Ledger files. Consequently, when the letters are printed, the field data will differ from customer to customer. The text shown with the normal background is common to all letters.

To create such a letter, simply type the text bits in from the keyboard and select the available fields by pressing function key **F4** and choosing from the list available. Figure 5.6 shows how function key F4 displays on the right-hand side of the screen the available fields that can be inserted into the letter.

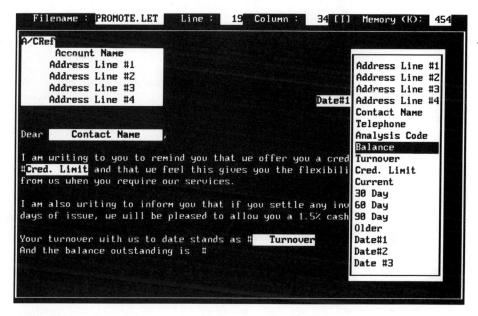

Fig 5.6

The resulting letter is shown in Fig 5.7. This letter clearly needs altering before it can be sent out – for example, 'Dear Jane Brown' should be corrected to 'Dear Ms Brown'. To print the letter you would return to the Sales Ledger and use the **Letters** option, in the same way as you did when you printed letters to customers who were ·overdue on their payments. This time you would change the choices from before to suit your new requirements and alter the filename to the one created. Again, plenty of practice at this will prove extremely useful as it allows you much greater flexibility in what you can get the computer to do for a business.

On a final point in this section, Sage does produce stationery that exactly fits the letters Sage has created. There is no reason why a business cannot have its own stationery with its own details already printed on it.

MANAGING THE PURCHASE LEDGER

Many of the advanced activities in the Purchase Ledger are exactly the same as for the Sales Ledger and will require little, if any, explanation.

Opening balances

As with operating the Sales Ledger for the first time, the Purchase Ledger will need to be set up with all supplier details and their opening balances before the Purchase Ledger can be used on a day-to-day basis.

0060
Howes Gym Centre
12 Spring Avenue
Bexley
London

30079X

Dear Jane Brown

I am writing to you to remind you that we offer you a credit limit of £ 300.00 and that we feel this gives you the flexibility to order from us when you require our services.

I am also writing to inform you that if you settle any invoices within 20 days of issue, we will be pleased to allow you a 1.5% cash discount.

Your Turnover with us to date is	£	340.00
And the balance outstanding is	£	399.50

Yours sincerely

J Blake
Accounts Manager

Fig 5.7

The reason for this is that, if opening balances are not placed into such accounts, they will not accurately reflect what a business owes its suppliers. Entering such opening balances requires the following operations:

1   The Nominal Account code must be the code for the Suspense Account which Sage sets up as 0100

2   **Inv** entry should be O/Bal

3   **Details** entry should be Opening Balance

The effect of this is to credit the Creditors Control Account by the amount owed to suppliers and, if you used the single opening balance method, debit the Suspense Account by this amount.

Refunds

The option in the Purchase Ledger allows either the cancellation of cheques or invoices in the same way as it did for the Sales Ledger. Cancelling a cheque means you are reversing the process of paying the supplier by debiting the Bank Account and crediting the Creditors Control Account. This might arise because you entered the payment of a supplier twice in error or have made the mistake of actually paying a supplier twice and need to cancel a cheque. When doing this, you need to make sure that the cheque will not be cleared by the bank as the accounts you have with both your bank and supplier will then not agree with yours.

You may need to cancel an invoice previously entered. Such a need can arise when a business has received a replacement invoice because there were a large number of errors in the original one from the supplier. In this instance, it is best to cancel the invoice previously entered and enter the new one. Alternatively, an invoice may have been entered into the computer in error or entered twice.

Remittance advice notes

Many businesses may decide that they wish to send a remittance advice note with their payments. The option in the Purchase Ledger produces something similar to that in Figure 5.8. The information on the advice note assumes that you are using preprinted stationery available from Sage. The routine prints out details of what the business owes the supplier and forms a detailed account of what invoices have been received and what the business is settling with the supplier.

Many businesses will not use this option at all because they often receive statements of account from their suppliers and such documents sent with payments serve no useful purpose.

The remittance note prints out details of your business and of your supplier. It then prints details of each invoice, with figures at the bottom showing from left to right the amount outstanding from invoices received in *current* month, *1* month ago, *2* months ago, *3* months ago, and *more than 3* months.

MEGAXAN STERLING SPORTS
100 SAGE ROW
BUSINESS ACTIVITY CENTRE
NEWCASTLE-UPON-TYNE
NE88 9ZZ

Ideal Sportswear plc				P0010
120 Spring Gardens				
Hillingsworth				15089X
Northampton				
NN22				1

17079X   00209X   Shirts and Shorts   181.25

| 181.25 | 0.00 | 0.00 | 0.00 | 0.00 |

181.25

Fig 5.8

MANAGING THE NOMINAL LEDGER

Recurring entries

Many of the Nominal Ledger activities involve entering expense and revenue items as either cash or journal transactions. Most transactions will be routine and occur every month, such as the payment of rent or the depreciation of a particular asset. Sage allows the setting up of such recurring entries so that these can be automated. At this stage you will only set up the details regarding recurring entries rather than actually performing them. That will be done later when you look at month end routines.

From the Nominal Ledger you should select the **Recurring Entries** option. If there are any entries already made, they will be displayed on your screen. Figure 5.9 shows two such recurring entries set up.

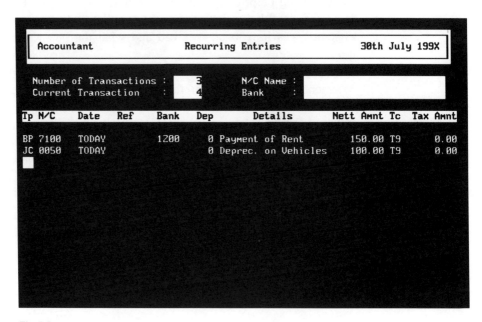

Fig 5.9

You are required to enter on each line details about recurring entries or amend existing ones. In the column headed **Tp** you enter one of the following transaction codes:

BP   Bank Payment
JD   Journal Debit
JC   Journal Credit
D   Delete the entry

The N/C column shows the Nominal account that has to be adjusted. In the case of Bank Payments, the Nominal account entered will be debited while the bank account is credited by the amount. This is confirmed in the Bank column which can be altered if you have more than one bank account reference.

The details entry is for documentation purposes only and helps make the audit trail easier to follow if the entry is good. The Nett Amount, Tax Code and Tax Amount columns are used to enter the details in the same way as any other transaction entry.

The important point to note is that you are simply setting up the system in preparation for future data processing rather than actually performing the entries. In the example shown in Figure 5.9 two such entries have been prepared where £150 is to paid out in rent and depreciation on vehicles of £100 is to be allowed for each time. These figures and lines can be altered at any time in the future.

Pressing **Esc** when you have finished will give you the option of posting the information to a file called RECUR.DTA which is used at a later stage by Sage. Such a system is typically used when expenses like rent are paid by Standing Order through a bank.

Prepayments

Many expenses that are paid for in any given month are not necessarily incurred in that month. For example, water rates may be paid twice yearly in advance. The effect on the accounts would be to suggest that water rates expenses were all incurred in the month that they were paid for. This would give a false impression of the profitability of the business for any given month. To get around this, Sage allows you to record only the actual part of the expense relevant to that month in the expense account, placing the remainder in a Prepayments Account. For example, if water rates costing £150 were paid in April for the next six months and the month is now June, then we would want the accounts to read as follows:

Account		Debit	Credit
Water Rates	Apr–Jun	£75	
Prepayment	Jul–Sep	£75	
Bank Account			£150

The water rates account is an expense and the prepayment account is a current asset.

To set up a prepayment, select **Prepayment and Accrual** from the Nominal Ledger menu and choose **PrePayments** from this menu. Figure 5.10 shows entries made for two such prepayments.

The **Name** field simply describes the nature of the Prepayment. The **N/C** column must be the account number of the expense that is prepaid. The first line in Figure 5.10 is the Rent Account and the second line is the Wages

Account. The **PRP** column is the current account code that holds the prepayment details.

```
┌─────────────────────────────────────────────────────────────────────┐
│  ┌─────────────────────────────────────────────────────────────────┐ │
│  │ Accountant              Prepayments            30th July 199X   │ │
│  └─────────────────────────────────────────────────────────────────┘ │
│                                                                       │
│    Number of Items :    2    N/C Name      :                          │
│    Current Item     :    3    Prepayment N/C :  ┌──────────────────┐  │
│                                                                       │
│   ┌─────────────────────────────────────────────────────────────────┐│
│   │ Name             N/C   PRP N/C Value     Mth Pst Monthly Jrn P    ││
│   └─────────────────────────────────────────────────────────────────┘│
│     Advance Rent paid  7100   1103    120.00   3   0      40.00        │
│     Advance Wages      7102   1103     30.00   3   0      10.00        │
│                                                                       │
│                                                                       │
│                                                                       │
│                                                                       │
│                                                                       │
│     Do you want to : [Post] Edit Abandon                              │
└─────────────────────────────────────────────────────────────────────┘
```

Fig 5.10

The **Value** is the amount that was actually paid and the **Mth** column shows how many months the payment covers. In the case of Rent, £120 has been paid and covers three months' rent. The remaining two fields are automatically done for you.

The **Pst** column shows the position in the current month. In both cases you are still in the first month with **0** months having elapsed. Consequently, the **Monthly Journal** figure shows one third appearing as the expense with the rest appearing in the prepayments account.

Later in this chapter you will see how the month end procedures automatically move the next amounts across to the expense account and gradually reduce the prepayments. Use of this function should be made each time an expense is prepaid. In other words, you will need to return to this the next time you pay your rates.

Accruals

The accruals work in almost exactly the same way as prepayments. Many expenses are not paid for when they are actually accrued. For example, electricity consumption is not actually paid for until a bill is received, which could be several months after much of it has been consumed. To get a better impression of what expenses are actually being accrued, you set up the details in the same way as you set up prepayments. There are many differences to prepayments however.

One main difference is that an accrual will show an expense that has not actually been paid for. Hence, as each month passes, the expense account has to be debited to the value of the accrual and an Accrued Expenses Account credited to show the money is owed. The Accrual Account forms a Current Liability on the Balance Sheet of the business. When the bill actually arrives, you will need to pay it to the accrual account rather than the expense account again. In other words, you credit the Bank Account in the usual way and debit the Accrual Account. If the bill is more than has been allowed for, then only the excess must be debited to the expense account.

To set up an accrual, select **Prepayment and Accrual** from the Nominal Ledger menu and choose **Accruals** from this menu. Entries are then carried out in the same way as for prepayments.

Depreciation

Depreciation has already been mentioned in the last chapter, but now you will deal with it in more detail as Sage has a useful way of helping you to set up depreciating procedures for the end of each month.

By selecting **Depreciation** from the Nominal Ledger you can set up the routines for monthly depreciation in the same way as you did for Recurring Entries, Prepayments and Accruals.

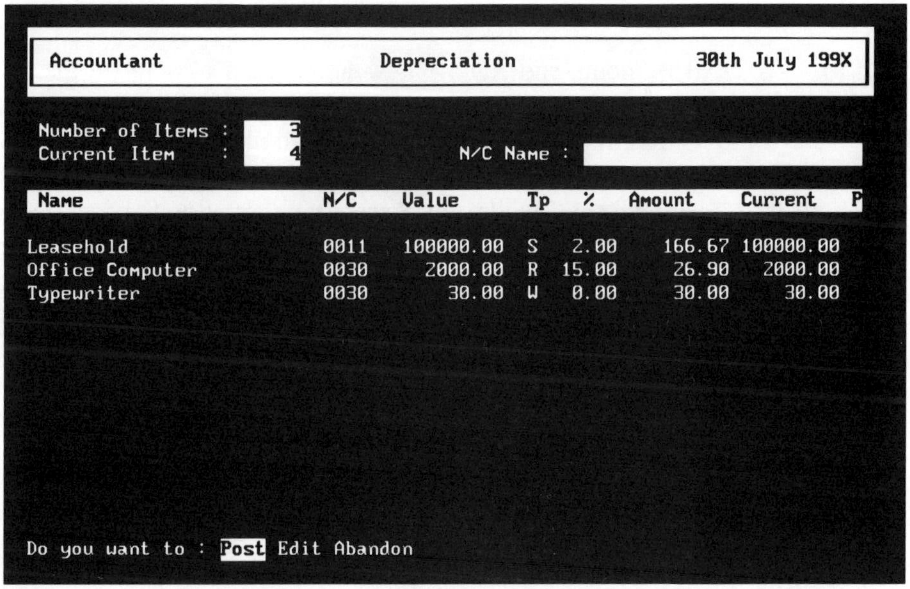

```
Accountant              Depreciation           30th July 199X

Number of Items :    3
Current Item    :    4          N/C Name :

Name            N/C   Value      Tp   %    Amount    Current   P

Leasehold       0011  100000.00  S   2.00  166.67 100000.00
Office Computer 0030    2000.00  R  15.00   26.90   2000.00
Typewriter      0030      30.00  W   0.00   30.00     30.00

Do you want to : Post Edit Abandon
```

Fig 5.11

The details entered are simply stored in a file and used later when certain end-of-month routines are run. The first column is **Name** which gives the name of the asset you are depreciating. The **N/C** is the nominal code where the asset cost is stored, while the **Value** column shows how much the asset cost when purchased.

The column **Tp** is used to indicate the type of depreciation, of which there are three:

S – Straight line This depreciates an asset value by the same amount each year in what is referred to as straight line depreciation. In the example shown in Figure 5.11 a leasehold valued at £100 000 is depreciated by 2% each year which amounts to £2000 per year. When divided by 12 to give a monthly value, it becomes £166.67 per month. Eventually, the asset will have no value.

R – Reducing balance This method of depreciation calculates depreciation on the last value of the asset rather than a percentage of the whole amount. For example, if a car is bought for £5000 and is depreciated by 20% per year, then a year's depreciation is calculated at £1000 (20% of £5000) leaving the car with a value of £4000. At the end of the second year, the depreciation becomes 20% of £4000 or £800. This method means most of the depreciation occurs in the earlier years of the life of an asset, which is usually fairly accurate for the value of cars, plant and equipment.

W – Writing off This writes off the value of an asset completely and is used when an asset has no value left at all.

Month end

The month-end routine now allows you to activate the four procedures that you have already set up. From the Sage **Utilities** menu you select **Month end**.

Recurring Entries will post all the transactions set up in your list of recurring entries. If the dates show TODAY then they will be posted with the system date, while those specifying dates will be posted with the specified dates. When carried out the report is similar to the one in Figure 5.12.

MEGAXAN STERLING SPORTS

Recurring Entries – Update Audit Trail   Date : 30079X

Page : 1

Tp	N/C	Date	Ref	Bank	Dep	Details	Nett	Tc	Tax
BP	7100	30079X		1200	0	Payment of Rent	150.00	T9	0.00
JC	0050	30079X			0	Deprec. on Vehicles	100.00	T9	0.00
JD	8000	30079X			0	Deprec. on Vehicles	100.00	T9	0.00

Fig 5.12

The report shows what nominal entries have been made as a result of running through the activity.

Prepayments & Accruals performs exactly the same actions on those set up. **Depreciation** will also have the effect of calculating and posting journal credits to each individual Accumulated Depreciation Account associated with each fixed asset and send a single balancing journal debit entry to the Depreciation expense account. The accumulated depreciation will appear in the Fixed Assets Accounts and the depreciation for that year will appear in the Profit & Loss Accounts.

Suspense accounts

A suspense account is an account that stores transaction figures that cannot be otherwise accounted for. For example, early in this chapter you offset the opening balances in customers' accounts against the Suspense Account. Hence, the Debtors Control Account would have been debited and the Suspense Account credited. At the end of the month, you will need to decide what to do with these Suspense Account entries, because they cannot remain in such accounts. In this example it may be decided that the balances represent sales of various kinds, in which case the sales accounts need to be credited and the Suspense Account debited to clear it.

Suspense accounts are often used when it is not known how to enter a figure. An operator can then get on with processing transactions quickly and return to the problem at a later stage; or give the problem to someone else!

VAT procedures

VAT, as mentioned in earlier chapters, is a tax on consumers rather than on a business. The tax is collected from sales and then passed on to HM Customs & Excise. Additionally, any VAT paid by a business can be claimed back from Customs & Excise. In practice, therefore, the difference between tax collected and tax paid is settled between a business and HM Customs & Excise.

Sage refers to tax collected in its reports as **Output** taxes, as these have to be paid out. Tax is calculated from sales invoices, sales credit notes, bank receipts and cash receipts. It is important that when the tax forms are completed the reports show how and when the tax was collected.

Sage refers to tax paid out in its reports as **Input** taxes, as these will be claimed back. Tax is calculated from purchase invoices, purchase credit notes, bank payments and cash payments.

All transactions that do not involve VAT, such as salaries and bank interest, should have been given the tax code **T9**.

At the end of the month, you should go through the process of clearing your VAT in preparation for future settlement. The effect will be to extract all VAT reports for a given month and determine whether you owe money to Customs & Excise or are owed money by them. To do this, you could undertake the following monthly routines:

1   Finish posting all transactions for the month. This can occupy a good deal of an operator's time trying to chase up invoices and receipts that have not yet been entered to the system.

2   Check the inputs and outputs by extracting a VAT Return report. This report is available from the Nominal Ledger and is divided into sections: Sales, Purchase, Nominal and Summary. The report shows the tax either collected or paid for each tax code T0 through to T9. When you extract the report it will also show the Nett value of Inputs and Outputs as well as the Tax amount.

The closing balance shown on the VAT Return Account must agree with the Trial Balance figure shown for Tax Control. If the Tax Control balance is a credit then it means that you owe that amount in VAT, while a debit balance shows you are owed the amount.

3   Correct any errors or omissions so that your VAT is correct. This may involve having to check invoices and other documents. A useful report to extract may be an Audit Trail giving details of all entries made in sequence of entry. The Audit Trail is available as the first activity in the Utilities function of Sage.

4   Carry out the month-end routines mentioned in the previous section. Some of these may affect the VAT figures.

5   Extract a final set of reports needed for VAT, namely the VAT Return report for the month in question only.

The next two stages will be used to clear the Tax Control Account of any balances left and is only a suggestion to help you to keep a month-by-month check on VAT liability. The idea is to set the VAT Control Account to zero and pass the figure across to a Tax Liability Account.

6   If the closing balance on the Tax Control account shows a *credit* balance then use the Journal Entry to:
Debit the Tax Control Account with the amount
Credit the Tax Liability Account with the amount

If the closing balance on the Tax Control account shows a *debit* balance then use the Journal Entry to:
Credit the Tax Control Account with the amount
Debit the Tax Liability Account with the amount

At this stage your Tax Control will have a zero balance to start the next month.

7   When you are ready to pay the VAT (assuming a credit balance), then you should complete the tax returns, which should be easy from the reports extracted. Then make a Bank Payment through the Nominal Ledger against the Tax Liability account.

Asset valuation

It is now worth seeing the effect the monthly end has had on the value of the fixed assets. From the Nominal Ledger menu you can select **Asset Valuation** and something similar to Figure 5.13 will appear.

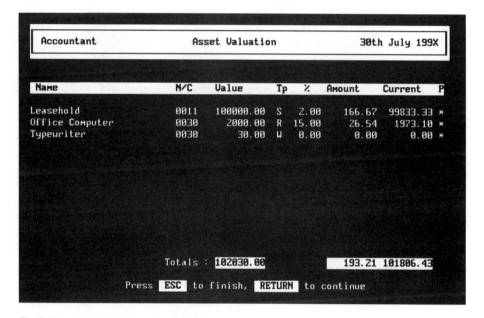

Name	N/C	Value	Tp	%	Amount	Current	P
Leasehold	0011	100000.00	S	2.00	166.67	99833.33	*
Office Computer	0030	2000.00	R	15.00	26.54	1973.10	*
Typewriter	0030	30.00	W	0.00	0.00	0.00	*

Accountant — Asset Valuation — 30th July 199X

Totals : 102030.00   193.21 101806.43

Press **ESC** to finish, **RETURN** to continue

Fig 5.13

The columns are similar to those set up when you entered details about depreciation. The Amount column shows the total accumulated depreciation while the Current column shows what the asset is worth. If no new assets are purchased, then the value of the assets will get progressively smaller as the months go on.

Monthly accounts

A useful feature of the Sage package is the ability to assess the business's performance and its status at the end of each month. The **Monthly Accounts** option from the Nominal Ledger allows you to see three important management reports, the Profit & Loss statement, the Balance Sheet and Budget report. To run this option, you are required to have at hand all the disks that hold the current trading year's accounts. Also, the option requires you to have set up your layout of accounts as described in the last chapter.

When you select this option it will process the transactions from the current month before asking you for a disk containing the transactions for previous months. Simply keep following the instructions until you have no more disks to put in. When you insert a blank disk, the reports will be produced.

The Profit & Loss report shows whether a profit has been made. It will be broken down into two sections. Firstly, the **Gross Profit** will show the profit made before overheads have been taken into account. Secondly, the **Nett Profit** is arrived at by deducting overheads and adding revenues.

The **Balance Sheet** will show the categories of Assets and Liabilities of the business along with how the assets of the business have been financed.

If you have been using the budget facilities, then the **Budget Report** will give a breakdown of what has actually been spent on these accounts along with what the budget was, and show the differences in the figures.

Conclusion and Exercises

As a way of gaining a greater knowledge and skill with the Ledgers, try the following questions.

1   **a**   Create four new Customer Accounts in the Sales Ledger and three new Supplier Accounts in the Purchase Ledger. Make sure that two of the accounts are the same so that a Contra Entry can be made later.

      b   Enter opening balances into each account.

      c   Extract a trial balance showing the amount that has been posted to the Suspense and Debtors' Control accounts.

      d   Now clear out the Suspense Account by using the Journal Entries facilities to post the amounts to the relevant Sales and Purchase Accounts.

2   Make a Contra Entry between two accounts of a customer who is also a supplier.

3   Process three returned cheques from customers where one is a refund and the other two are 'bounced' cheques.

4   Write off an account as a bad debt.

5   Mail a letter to all those suppliers to whom you own money, announcing that you now have a new telephone number for a new fax (facsimile) machine.

6   Pay a supplier a sum of money and issue a remittance advice note.

7   **a**   Using the examples set out in the chapter, set up the following recurring entries:
Bank payment by standing order for rent
Payments of wages by cheque

b Set up a prepayment for water rates and an accrual for electricity consumption.

c Carry out a month end activity to show the processing that results from **a** and **b**.

d Extract a Trial Balance showing the outcome of **c**.

6 Stock control

INTRODUCTION

In this chapter you will examine the way in which a computer records information about stock and how such information can assist a business in determining efficient management of stock. The work on the ledgers in this chapter is not available to Sage Bookkeeper or Accountant users but only available to **Accountant Plus** and **Financial Controller** users. In the following two chapters on invoicing and order processing, you will see further activities involving the stock control function.

An aim of controlling stock is to keep stock at its lowest level without impeding either sales or production. If a business holds more stock than is necessary for the running of the business, then the business may well find itself with an unnecessarily high cost for holding stock. For example, suppose you have invested £10 000 more in stock than is needed. This £10 000 if placed in a deposit account at a bank is capable of earning money in interest payments. However there are some advantages for certain businesses in holding high stocks.

The costs of holding stock include the cost of capital tied up in that stock, money that could be used elsewhere in the business. Also, for certain stock, such as frozen foods, there is a high cost of simply storing and looking after stock. With other types of stock, such as fashion wear, the stock can soon be obsolete if it is kept too long and not sold. For businesses such as green-grocers stocks have to be low because goods will perish or become unsaleable in a short time.

On the other hand, holding large stocks can have real benefits. One benefit can be that the cost of capital tied up in stock can be paid for by the rising value of stock through inflation. Holding high stocks for this purpose can be risky if the value of stock fluctuates a great deal. Often businesses derive the benefit of being able to supply customers quickly and at short notice if their stocks are high, sales which might otherwise be lost. Stock of certain items may be high because there are large quantity discounts available from suppliers.

The efficient levels of stock that should be held by a business will vary quite considerably from one to another. Sage Stock Control will not be able to make decisions about what represents efficient stock levels. You will have to give the computer this information. What the computer will do is to advise you, with its reporting facilities, of what stock either needs replacing or is too high.

THE STRUCTURE OF SAGE STOCK CONTROL

The Stock Control function can be broken down into three broad areas:

1   The need to set up the stock records that hold information about description, cost, selling price, how stock is sold, when to re-order more stock and how much to order. These records need to be set up for each stock item.

2   The day-to-day updating of stock. Every time stock is sold, the quantity has to be deducted from the stock held. Also, the stock records will need to keep a check on what replacement stock has been ordered and whether any has already been allocated to customers.

3   The reports needed to help a business keep adequate stock levels and give it information about what stock has been selling fast or slowly.

The Stock Control function is shown in Fig 6.1.

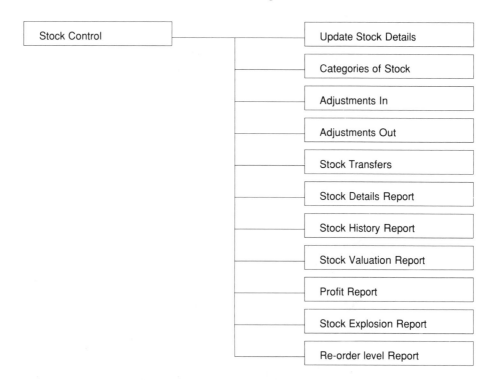

```
Stock Control ────────┬──────── Update Stock Details
                      ├──────── Categories of Stock
                      ├──────── Adjustments In
                      ├──────── Adjustments Out
                      ├──────── Stock Transfers
                      ├──────── Stock Details Report
                      ├──────── Stock History Report
                      ├──────── Stock Valuation Report
                      ├──────── Profit Report
                      ├──────── Stock Explosion Report
                      └──────── Re-order level Report
```

Fig 6.1

Extra functions ʰhat directly affect stock are left until the next two chapters. The invoicing function will have the effect of altering stock. When customers are invoiced, it will remove from stock the goods they are invoiced for. Also, Sales Order Processing will have the effect of *allocating* stock to a customer. In addition to this, Purchase Orders will inform the Stock Control function about what stock is on order.

PREPARING STOCK RECORDS

The first job you will need to undertake is to set up details on every item of stock. This can be a major undertaking for a business computerising Stock Control for the first time as it can involve many hundreds of items of stock. The way Sage stores details about stock is to organise stock into categories. For example, a jeweller may have a category for watches, one for clocks, another for rings and so on. Into each category will go details on individual items of stock. After this has been done, the actual quantities in stock will have to entered. Figure 6.2 gives an outline of the stages in preparing the Stock Control function.

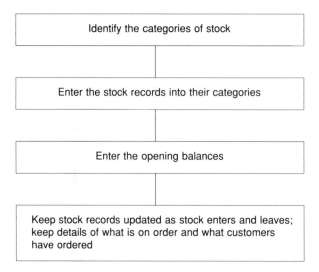

Fig 6.2

From the main Stock Control menu, select **Categories** to set up the first stage. Figure 6.3 shows an example of categories set up for the stock records to be inserted.

Although categories can be added, altered or deleted in the future, it is important to note that each stock record is identified with a category number. If you feel you do not need to divide your stock into categories, then you can ignore this activity and all stock will be assumed to be category 1.

```
┌──────────────────────────────────────────────────────────────────┐
│ Accountant Plus              Categories          18th August 199X  │
└──────────────────────────────────────────────────────────────────┘

            Category  Name   1    :  Sports Clothing
               ..      ..     2    :  Cricket Supplies
               ..      ..     3    :  Soccer Supplies
               ..      ..     4    :  Rugby Supplies
               ..      ..     5    :  Golf Supplies
               ..      ..     6    :  Tennis Supplies
               ..      ..     7    :
               ..      ..     8    :
               ..      ..     9    :
               ..      ..    10    :
               ..      ..    11    :
               ..      ..    12    :
               ..      ..    13    :
               ..      ..    14    :
               ..      ..    15    :
```

Fig 6.3

The next stage is to enter details of stock. From the Stock Control menu
you should select **Update Stock Details**. You will see a blank form on the
screen which needs to have some of the details completed. Each detail is a
field, making up the stock record. Some of the fields are left for future
processing. Figure 6.4 shows an example of a stock record prepared with the
opening fields.

```
┌──────────────────────────────────────────────────────────────────┐
│ Accountant Plus           Update Stock Details   18th August 199X  │
└──────────────────────────────────────────────────────────────────┘

 Stock Code     : 00010              Do you want to : Post Abandon Delete

 Description    : T-Shirt - Medium Red/White      In Stock     :      0.00
 Category       :  1                              On Order     :      0.00
 Category Name  : Sports Clothing                 Allocated    :      0.00
                                                  Make Up      :      0.00
 Sale Price     :    12.95
 Cost Price     :     0.00                     Quantity Sold Mth :    0.00
 Unit of Sale   : 1                            Quantity Sold YTD :    0.00

 Re-order level :    20.00                     Value Sold Mth :      0.00
 Re-order qty   :    10.00                     Value Sold YTD :      0.00

 Discount A %   :        10.00                    Last Sale        :
 Discount B %   :        15.00                    Last Purchase    :
 Discount C %   :        20.00
 Nominal Code   : 4000                         Supplier     : P0010
 Department     :    0                         Part Ref.    : T-Shirt Med R/W
 Tax Code       : T1                           Location     :
```

Fig 6.4

In this option, there is no need to concern ourselves with the amount in stock, just the details about an item of stock. **Stock Code** represents the way an item of stock is identified and must be unique to each item of stock. The **Description** describes the item using up to 30 characters. The **Category** is the category number set up earlier. You can select the category by using the function key **F4** to choose from a list. The Category name is inserted for you. The **Sale Price** is the price at which you sell each unit, with **Unit of Sale** being how many items you sell at that price. You will not be asked for **Cost Price** until you enter some opening stock.

The **Re-order Level** is the stock level at which, when reached, a purchase order should be placed. This is going to be crucial for assisting a business in keeping a check that adequate stocks are maintained. One of the reporting facilities will need this information to establish what should be ordered at any given time. If this is left blank, the re-order level check will not be performed. The **Re-order quantity** is the amount that is normally ordered once the re-order level has been reached.

The next three lines are the three **Discount** figures. These entries are optional but will assist the sales ordering process, as you will see in Chapter 8. When a customer places an order and you enter the details into the computer, you will have the option of selecting one of these discount rates on the stock ordered.

The **Nominal Code** is needed if you are to integrate the invoicing with stock and the Sales Ledger. The nominal code will refer to the nominal account that is to be used when a sale is made. It is a good idea to have nominal codes matching the categories of stock. For example, if you have six stock categories all named, then it would make your work much easier if you had exactly the same number of nominal sales accounts that were given the same names. You can use function key F4 to select from the list of nominal accounts.

The **Department** code is similar to that of the nominal code in that it is only used if you are using departmental analysis and integrating Stock Control with Invoicing, Sales Ledger and Nominal Ledger. Again you can use function key F4 to select from the list of departments.

Tax Code is used to integrate with the invoicing and Sales Ledger. The code will be the VAT code (T0, T1, etc.) that is associated with this item of stock.

The only other details that need completing at this stage are the supplier details at the end of the form. The **Supplier Code** can be used to indicate who normally supplies the stock item. You can use function key F4 to select from the list of supplier accounts. The **Part Ref** is the part reference used by your supplier for them to identify stock. This reference will appear on future Purchase Orders sent to suppliers. The **Location** is again used to help the supplier when orders are sent to them.

At this point you should press **Esc** and **Post** the record to the stock file. If, however, the stock item you have entered is an assembly of other stock items, it will require a little more processing. At the end of this chapter, there is a list of suggested stock items which this book has used and this may help you to build up some stock records to work with.

STOCK ASSEMBLY

Many stock items may be an **assembly** of other stock items. For example, if you work in a television factory, then a television set, when completed, forms a part of your finished stock. Meanwhile, the components of the television set are also stored in stock as either semi-finished goods or raw materials.

Sage will allow you to define an assembly. In future processing you are then able to increase the number of finished goods in stock and all the required semi-finished stock and raw material stock to make the finished goods is removed from stock. Sage will also calculate for you how many of the finished stock you can make from existing stocks.

From the Stock Control Menu you select **Update Stock Details** and enter the first screen in exactly the same way as you would any other stock item. When you have entered the initial details, instead of pressing Esc and posting the details, press the **Page Down** on your keyboard to get the **Component Assembly** screen. Figure 6.5 shows an example of how a stock called 'Tennis Play Kit' is made up of two components of stock.

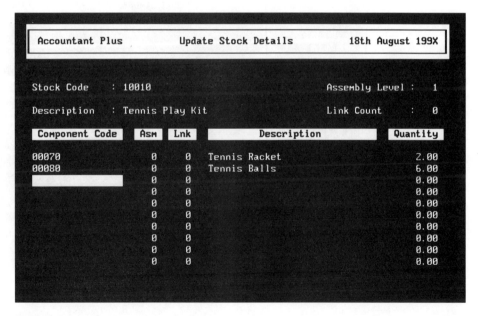

Fig 6.5

Constructing a complete stock database can be a very long process for a business and needs careful planning. In Chapter 10 you will have a chance to consider how a business may go about this in a practical way.

STOCK MOVEMENTS

The next step is to examine stock movements. Stock movements are recorded through the Stock Control system using the **Adjustments In** and **Adjustments Out** options. If integrated with Invoicing and Sales Order Processing, then the issue of an invoice will result in automatic adjustment of stock, thereby avoiding the need to record a stock movement in this section. Also, when goods are received after a Purchase Order has been issued, the acknowledgement of this must be recorded both as a stock movement and within the purchase order system, a topic to be covered in Chapter 8.

Before you can start using the Stock Control function for recording movements of stock, you will need to enter an opening balance. In practice, a business will need to do a complete stock take at a given point in time and enter all the details immediately. This can be a complicated affair as speed is of the essence. If a business is too slow in entering the details into the computer, the stock quantities can be badly out of date before you finish.

To enter an opening stock, select **Adjustments In** from the Stock Control menu and select the stock code for which you want to enter opening stock. Figure 6.6 shows an example of an entry.

```
┌──────────────────────────────────────────────────────────────────────┐
│  Accountant Plus              Adjustments In           18th August 199X │
└──────────────────────────────────────────────────────────────────────┘


    Stock Code      : 00090          Do you want to : Post Edit Abandon

    Description     : Soccer Ball

    Quantity        :    28.00                Qty in Stock   :    0.00
                                              Qty Allocated  :    0.00
    Cost Price      :    12.00                Qty On-Order   :    0.00
    Sale Price      :    18.00

    Narrative       : Opening Stock

    Reference       : O/Bal                   Last Sale      :
    Date            : 18089X                  Last Purchase  :
```

Fig 6.6

You can select the stock code using function key F4. The **Description** is shown automatically for you. The **Quantity** should be the amount of opening stock, with the **Cost price** being the cost for each individual item of stock. If you purchased your existing stock at more than one price, then you should make a separate entry for each cost price. This is used later to assess how much profit you have been making in buying and selling the stock. Figure 6.6

shows an opening stock balance having been entered and ready for posting to the stock file.

The cost price of the stock has been entered as £12 while the selling price of £18 is already there from when the stock record was created. Consequently, the entry shows that we start off with 28 soccer balls in stock each costing £12.

If you are not using the invoice system for recording stock issues, then each time stock is issued or despatched to a customer, you should record this movement as an **Adjustment Out**. The Narrative field would then be used to reflect something about the invoice that was sent or something like **Cash Sales**. The reference would be used to record the invoice number or receipt number.

As stock is received, you would enter details into the stock system using **Adjustments In**. Again, the narrative could be the supplier's name and the reference the supplier's invoice number.

It is important that entries of stock movement are made as soon as possible after the event has occurred. Failure to do so will render the reports meaningless.

EXTRACTING REPORTS

Once some stock processing has been done, you are soon able to extract some useful management information about stock. Figure 6.7 shows the details of the 'Tennis Play Kit' that was set up with components earlier. This report can be accessed using **Stock Details** from the Stock Control menu.

```
┌─────────────────────────────────────────────────────────────────────┐
│  ┌──────────────────────────────────────────────────────────────┐   │
│  │ Accountant Plus          Stock Details          18th August 199X │   │
│  └──────────────────────────────────────────────────────────────┘   │
│                                                                       │
│   Stock Code      : 10010              In Stock      :     3.00       │
│   Description     : Tennis Play Kit    On Order      :     0.00       │
│   Category        : 6                  Allocated     :     0.00       │
│   Category Name   : Tennis Supplies    Make Up       :    15.83       │
│                                                                       │
│   Sale Price      :    50.00           Quantity Sold Mth :   0.00     │
│   Cost Price      :     0.00           Quantity Sold YTD :   0.00     │
│   Unit of Sale    : 1                                                 │
│   Re-order level  :     5.00           Value Sold Mth :     0.00      │
│   Re-order qty    :     0.00           Value Sold YTD :     0.00      │
│                                                                       │
│   Discount A %    :      5.00          Last Sale         :            │
│   Discount B %    :      7.50          Last Purchase     :            │
│   Discount C %    :     10.00                                         │
│   Nominal Code    : 4101               Supplier     :                 │
│   Department      : 0                  Part Ref.    :                 │
│   Tax Code        : T1                 Location     :                 │
│                                                                       │
│      Press  ESC  to finish,  RETURN  to continue,  →  for Assembly Details │
└─────────────────────────────────────────────────────────────────────┘
```

Fig 6.7

It shows that there are three kits currently in stock and, if you look at the **Make Up** field, it shows there are also sufficient components in stock to make up a further 15.83 of the kits (15 in reality).

You can also get a complete history of stock movement using the **Stock History** option Stock Control. Such a report is useful when you are trying to get some idea about how sales of certain stocks are performing. Another useful report available is the **Valuation of Stock**. Figure 6.8 shows an excerpt from such a report. This report also allows you the option of breaking the report into categories.

MEGAXAN STERLING SPORTS Stock Reports – Stock Valuation

Category : 1 : Sports Clothing

Stock Code	Stock Description	Quantity in Stock	Average Unit Cost	Stock Value	Selling Price	Expected Sales
00010	T-Shirt – Medium Red/White	45.00	9.00	405.00	12.95	582.75
00020	T-Shirts Small Red/White	30.00	9.00	270.00	12.50	375.00
00030	T-Shirts Large Red/White	30.00	8.00	240.00	13.78	413.40
00040	Scarves	2.00	4.00	8.00	9.99	19.98
			Total:	923.00		1391.13

Fig 6.8

The Average Unit Cost is calculated by taking the total amount for the existing stock and dividing it by the quantity in stock. The expected sales value is calculated as the selling price multiplied by the quantity in stock. It does not take account of discounts given to customers.

Another report called **Stock Explosion** shows how certain stock records are broken down into components. Figure 6.9 shows such a report viewed on the screen.

To get to this screen select the report and ask to **View** it. The computer will then create a temporary report file called report.**???** where the question marks are numbers. It writes the report to this file which you will then view. You can use the cursor keys to move around the screen to see all of the report. When you have finished viewing the report, press the **Esc** key and you are given a choice of what you want done with the report. If you **Quit** the report at this stage the report will be removed from the computer. To **View** the file keeps you with the screen. If you choose to **Save** it, it will give the report the name already created. If you **Print** the file, make sure your printer is ready before selecting the option.

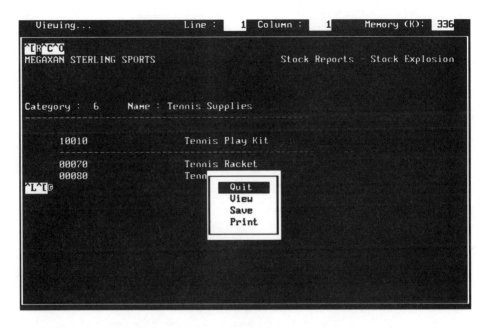

Fig 6.9

STOCK TRANSFERS

The option **Stock Transfers** allows you to add to finished stock from the components. Figure 6.10 shows an example of this.

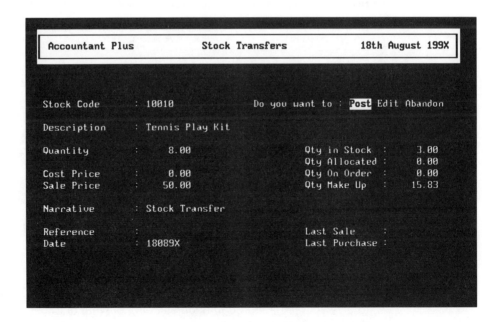

Fig 6.10

In the example, the information about this stock, once chosen, shows up to 15 kits can be made. By selecting to make 8 kits, it will add these to the stock of 3 making 11 in total and remove all the components from the other stock records. As each kit comprised 2 tennis rackets and 6 tennis balls, for the 8 new kits it will remove a total of 16 tennis rackets and 48 tennis balls from those stock items. This has to done because if stock were not removed from the other records, the stock valuation report would show stock being counted twice and giving a valuation of stock that is too high.

If you attempt this, then it is worth investigating stock history, valuation of stock and stock details in order to see the effect of the action.

RE-ORDERING STOCK

When you created the stock records, you also entered re-order levels into one of the fields. These re-order levels are suggested stock levels at which, when reached, you should put in a purchase order for more stock. The re-order levels should take account of the time it takes from placing an order with a supplier to the stock getting to you; this time taken is called the *lead time* and, generally, the longer the lead time, the higher will be re-order level. Another factor that needs to be considered is the quantity sold. If the average stock held will clear in a few days then you need to re-order early enough so as not to run out of stock.

The re-order report will collect details about all items that have a quantity in stock below their re-order level. Figure 6.11 shows such a report.

MEGAXAN STERLING SPORTS   Stock Reports – re-order levels

Stock Code	Description	Quantity In Stock	Quantity Allocate	Quantity On-Order	Re-Order Level	Re-Order Quantity	Purchase Price	P/C
00040	Scarves	2.00	0.00	0.00	20.00	15.00	4.00	P0010
00050	Cricket Pads	5.00	0.00	0.00	30.00	12.00	9.65	P0030
00060	Cricket Bats – Large	9.00	0.00	0.00	20.00	10.00	20.00	P0020

Fig 6.11

All the details have been extracted from the stock records. The re-order quantity was entered when the records were created. Such quantities have to take into account any quantity discounts available to you as well as how much you sell of this item of stock.

The Quantity Allocated and Quantity On-Order will be discussed in Chapter 8.

Exercises

As a conclusion to this chapter on stock, try the following exercises in order to give yourself a thorough understanding of what activities are available with the Stock Control function.

1   Create another 10 stock records and enter opening stocks for them, adding one new category of stock to the list of categories already made up.

2   Add two more stock records that are made up of components from other stock records.

3   Make some adjustments in and out to at least 12 of the records in order to build some history for these stocks.

4   Perform a transfer of stock to one of the stock items which is made up from stock components.

5   Now extract the following reports:

Stock Details
Stock History
Valuation of Stock
Stock Explosion
Re-order levels

Appendix

The following stock records are the basis for this chapter and have been limited to keep the book to a realistic size. You are advised to add some of your own to this list.

MEGAXAN STERLING SPORTS – stock details

Category : 1 : Sports Clothing

Stock Code	: 00010	In-Stock	: 35.00	Units of Sale	: 1
Stock Desc.	: T-Shirt – Medium Red/White	On-Order	: 0.00	Sup. Part Ref.	: T-Shirt Med R/W
Department Code :	0	Allocated	: 0.00	Supplier Code	: P0010
Tax Code	: T1	Bin Location	:	Purchase Price :	9.00
Nominal Code	: 4000	Discount Rate A : 10.00	Selling Price	12.95
Re-order Level	: 20.00	Discount Rate B : 15.00	Date Last Pur. :
Re-order Qty	: 10.00	Discount Rate C : 20.00	Date Last Sale : 180891

Stock Code	: 00020	In-Stock	: 24.00	Units of Sale	: 1
Stock Desc.	: T-Shirts Small Red/White	On-Order	: 0.00	Sup. Part Ref.	: T-Shirt Med R/W
Department Code :	0	Allocated	: 0.00	Supplier Code	: P0010
Tax Code	: T1	Bin Location	:	Purchase Price :	9.00
Nominal Code	: 4000	Discount Rate A : 10.00	Selling Price	12.50
Re-order Level	: 15.00	Discount Rate B : 15.00	Date Last Pur. :
Re-order Qty	: 10.00	Discount Rate C : 20.00	Date Last Sale : 180891

Stock Code	: 00030	In-Stock	: 29.00	Units of Sale	: 1
Stock Desc.	: T-Shirts Large Red/White	On-Order	: 0.00	Sup. Part Ref.	: T-Shirt Lrg R/W
Department Code :	0	Allocated	: 0.00	Supplier Code	: P0010
Tax Code	: T1	Bin Location	:	Purchase Price :	8.00
Nominal Code	: 4000	Discount Rate A : 10.00	Selling Price	13.78
Re-order Level	: 15.00	Discount Rate B : 15.00	Date Last Pur. :
Re-order Qty	: 10.00	Discount Rate C : 20.00	Date Last Sale : 180891

Stock Code : 00040	In-Stock : 1.00	Units of Sale : 1
Stock Desc. : Scarves	On-Order : 0.00	Sup. Part Ref. : Scarves
Department Code : 0	Allocated : 0.00	Supplier Code : P0010
Tax Code : T1	Bin Location :	Purchase Price : 4.00
Nominal Code : 4000	Discount Rate A : 10.00	Selling Price : 9.99
Re-order Level : 20.00	Discount Rate B : 15.00	Date Last Pur. :
Re-order Qty : 15.00	Discount Rate C : 20.00	Date Last Sale : 180891

Category : 2 : Cricket Supplies

Stock Code : 00050	In-Stock : 5.00	Units of Sale : Pair
Stock Desc. : Cricket Pads	On-Order : 0.00	Sup. Part Ref. : C-P332
Department Code : 0	Allocated : 0.00	Supplier Code : P0030
Tax Code : T1	Bin Location :	Purchase Price : 9.65
Nominal Code : 4001	Discount Rate A : 10.00	Selling Price : 15.00
Re-order Level : 30.00	Discount Rate B : 15.00	Date Last Pur. :
Re-order Qty : 12.00	Discount Rate C : 20.00	Date Last Sale :

Stock Code : 00060	In-Stock : 9.00	Units of Sale : 1
Stock Desc. : Cricket Bats – Large	On-Order : 0.00	Sup. Part Ref. : 6376272
Department Code : 0	Allocated : 0.00	Supplier Code : P0020
Tax Code : T1	Bin Location :	Purchase Price : 20.00
Nominal Code : 4001	Discount Rate A : 10.00	Selling Price : 32.00
Re-order Level : 20.00	Discount Rate B : 15.00	Date Last Pur. :
Re-order Qty : 10.00	Discount Rate C : 20.00	Date Last Sale :

Category : 3 : Soccer Supplies

Stock Code : 00090	In-Stock : 28.00	Units of Sale : 1
Stock Desc. : Soccer Ball	On-Order : 0.00	Sup. Part Ref. : SB93382
Department Code : 0	Allocated : 0.00	Supplier Code : P0040
Tax Code : T1	Bin Location :	Purchase Price : 12.00
Nominal Code : 4002	Discount Rate A : 5.00	Selling Price : 18.00
Re-order Level : 12.00	Discount Rate B : 10.00	Date Last Pur. :
Re-order Qty : 5.00	Discount Rate C : 15.00	Date Last Sale :

Category : 6 : Tennis Supplies

Stock Code : 00070	In-Stock : 24.00	Units of Sale : 1
Stock Desc. : Tennis Racket	On-Order : 0.00	Sup. Part Ref. : TR512
Department Code : 0	Allocated : 0.00	Supplier Code : P0050
Tax Code : T1	Bin Location :	Purchase Price : 20.00
Nominal Code : 4101	Discount Rate A : 10.00	Selling Price : 26.00
Re-order Level : 25.00	Discount Rate B : 15.00	Date Last Pur. :
Re-order Qty : 12.00	Discount Rate C : 20.00	Date Last Sale :

Stock Code : 00080	In-Stock : 47.00	Units of Sale : 1
Stock Desc. : Tennis Balls	On-Order : 0.00	Sup. Part Ref. : 766211
Department Code : 0	Allocated : 0.00	Supplier Code : P0050
Tax Code : T1	Bin Location :	Purchase Price : 0.80
Nominal Code : 4101	Discount Rate A : 5.00	Selling Price : 1.20
Re-order Level : 50.00	Discount Rate B : 7.50	Date Last Pur. :
Re-order Qty : 20.00	Discount Rate C : 10.00	Date Last Sale :

Stock Code : 10010	In-Stock : 11.00	Units of Sale : 1
Stock Desc. : Tennis Play Kit	On-Order : 0.00	Sup. Part Ref. :
Department Code : 0	Allocated : 0.00	Supplier Code :
Tax Code : T1	Bin Location :	Purchase Price : 44.80
Nominal Code : 4101	Discount Rate A : 5.00	Selling Price : 50.00
Re-order Level : 5.00	Discount Rate B : 7.50	Date Last Pur. :
Re-order Qty : 0.00	Discount Rate C : 10.00	Date Last Sale :

7 Sales invoicing

INTRODUCTION

The main objectives of sales invoicing are to produce invoices and credit notes as well as to maintain up-to-date stock files and customer records. The activities in this chapter are not available to Sage Bookkeeper or Accountant users but are available to **Accountant Plus** and **Financial Controller** users.

Until now, you have been processing sales invoices in a somewhat unusual manner, invoice details having been directly entered to the Sales Ledger with all invoice details required, but with no invoices! One of the principal objectives of this chapter, therefore, is to produce invoices automatically, extracting all the customer information from the Sales Ledger and performing all calculations automatically, including totals and VAT. Ultimately, you want the computer to update the Sales Ledger automatically, rather than for you to post invoices one at a time through the Sales Ledger. Consequently, this part of the Sage package requires integration with both the Sales Ledger function and Stock Control function.

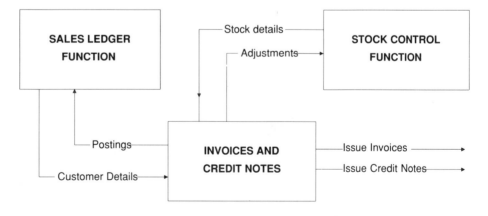

Fig 7.1

Figure 7.1 depicts the way the Invoicing and Credit Note functions are integrated with other functions. Each invoice will extract from the Sales Ledger the details about the customer who is to receive the invoice. When the invoice is despatched with the goods, the customer records will be updated with the details of the invoice. Also, each invoice and credit note will need to extract from the stock file details about the stock being sold, and subsequently stock files will need updating to show the goods were sold.

THE STRUCTURE OF THE INVOICING FUNCTION

The Sales Invoicing function is accessed via the Sales Ledger. From the Sales Ledger menu select **Invoice Production** to get to the activities available within this function. Later in the chapter, you will see how to enter into the Utilities function in order to alter the stationery layouts needed to print an invoice in a format to suit your business. The activities in the function are set out in Fig 7.2.

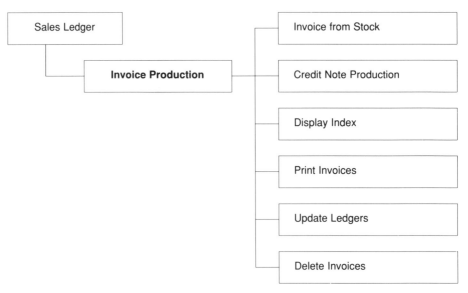

Fig 7.2

PREPARING DOCUMENTS

When generating invoices, you will find that most of the work has already been done when you set up the customer details in the Sales Ledger and the stock details in Stock Control. The principle of invoicing is that you first produce all the details of an invoice and store these details in a file. Later, you will print the invoices when they are needed. After checking them through, make any amendments and then print off the invoices. When all the invoices have been printed, they are ready to be despatched with the goods. The final stage in the process will be to post the details to both the Sales Ledger and Stock Control.

To produce an invoice using the details held in stock, select from the

Invoice Production menu the option **Invoicing from Stock**. There are three stages to producing an invoice. The first stage is to enter on the first screen details about who is to receive the invoice. Sage refers to this as the **Header** page.

The first page really concerns itself with who the invoice is for and how the goods are to be sent. The **Invoice Number** is generated by the computer starting from 1 and increasing this by 1 each time – you can start with a different number by altering it yourself. The **Sales Ref** field is the Customer Account number as it appears in the Sales Ledger. When this number is entered, the activity extracts the customer information from the Sales Ledger. You can select the customer by pressing function key **F4** and selecting the customer from the list available on the Sales Ledger. The **Date** will automatically display the system date, which can be changed.

The Customer Name, Address and Telephone, although extracted from the Sales Ledger, can be altered if you so wish. In addition to this the Delivery Name and Address can be typed in if it is different from the Customer Name and Address.

The **Order No** is used if the customer has previously placed an order for the goods. More will be said on this in Chapter 8. For many businesses, the invoice will be based on an order previously placed with it (here you can use whatever number you care to give it). The customer order number will be the number on the purchase order sent by the customer.

The Total Nett, Total Tax, Total Gross and Early Payment will be calculated for you when you enter the details about the stock to be invoiced.

The next stage is to move to the second screen and start putting in stock details. This is arrived at by pressing the **Page Down** key. The second page now appears with information required on the actual goods to be sent and about prices, VAT and the amount to be paid. For each stock line sent, you will have to complete this page. Figure 7.3 gives an example of an entry.

```
┌─────────────────────────────────────────────────────────────────────┐
│ Accountant Plus         Invoicing from Stock       18th August 199X   │
└─────────────────────────────────────────────────────────────────────┘

 Invoice No.   :       1                    Total Nett   :      96.00
 Customer      : Wantworth Cricket Club     Total Tax    :      16.80
 Item No.      :       1                    Total Gross  :     112.80

 Stock Code    : 00050
 Description   : Cricket Pads
 Comment 1     :
     ..   2    :

 Quantity      :       8.00
                                    Exceeds Current Stock levels :    5.00
 Units        °: Pair               Available Stock to make up   :    0.00
 Unit Price    : 15.00
                                            Cost       :      120.00
 Discount %    :      20.00                 Discount   :       24.00
 Tax Code      : T1                         Subtotal   :       96.00
 Tax Value %   :      17.50                 Tax        :       16.80
 Nominal Code  : 4001
 Department    :       0                     TOTAL      :      112.80
```

Fig 7.3

The **Stock Code** will be the first field required. The stock code is a code that must exist in the stock file. You can use function key F4 to select the item of stock. When selected the activity then searches the stock file to find the required details on a product. The **Description** will be found automatically from the stock file, but can be altered if desired. Two comment lines can be used to enter any details about the product which you want to draw to the attention of the customer.

The **Quantity** entered is the number of units required. If you attempt to invoice for more stock than you actually have, a message will appear on the screen to this effect and tell you what available stock you actually have. The **Unit Price** will be found automatically from the stock file, and this too can be altered if desired.

The **Discount** available on a particular line can be selected from one of the discounts stored with the stock record in the stock file. You are given A, B or C to choose from. You can, if you wish, put in a zero discount or a different one altogether.

The **Tax Code** for this item is also extracted from the stock file and can be changed. Likewise, the tax rate (value) is shown as that for the tax code which has been stored in the tax tables.

The Nominal Code is going to be important at a later stage when the details of the sale are posted to the Nominal Ledger. The code given here shows where the Nett Total amount will be posted. The code should, therefore, be one of the Sales Accounts set up in the Nominal Ledger. If the stock file has been given a nominal code then this nominal code will be entered for you.

The Department code can be selected if the sale is to be allocated to a particular department. The department code should also be in the stock file and will be displayed for you automatically.

The details down the right-hand side of the screen are used for information purposes only. The Total Nett figure is the accumulated total so far of all the goods on the invoice; likewise the tax. The Total Gross is the two figures added up. In the bottom right-hand corner you have the totals on this stock line only. The **Cost** figure is found by multiplying the quantity issued by the unit price ($8 \times £15 = £120$). The discount was calculated from what was chosen (20% of £120 being £24). The subtotal, therefore, is the amount after the discount. It is this total that must be recorded in the Sales Ledger and Nominal Ledger. Also the tax is calculated on the subtotal figure (17.5% of £96 is £16.80).

Once this screen is completed, you should press the **Page Down** key on your keyboard to enter details of the next stock line ordered. You should keep doing this for each item of stock ordered. You are allowed as many stock lines as you like. If too many stock lines are entered to fit on a page, the system will generate continuation pages for you.

The only essential details you need to enter for the stock lines are Stock Code and Quantity. All the rest can be extracted from the stock file if it has been properly set up. This can make invoicing extremely fast and accurate.

When each stock line has been entered you should press **Page Down** again from a blank stock line page. The final page is used to store **footer** details and an example of this appears in Fig 7.4.

```
┌──────────────────────────────────────────────────────────────────┐
│ ┌──────────────────────────────────────────────────────────────┐ │
│ │ Accountant Plus          Invoicing from Stock     18th August 199X │ │
│ └──────────────────────────────────────────────────────────────┘ │
│                                                                    │
│  Invoice No. :      1              Tax Code     : T1               │
│  Customer    : Wantworth Cricket Club   Tax %    :        17.50    │
│                                                                    │
│  Notes 1     : Please note there is a   Nominal Code  : 4002       │
│  ..    2     : cash discount available  Department    :    0       │
│  ..    3     : for prompt payment       Description   :            │
│                                                                    │
│                                                                    │
│  Items Nett  :       147.20  Carriage :     5.00  Total Nett  :      152.20 │
│                              Tax Code : T1                         │
│                              Tax %    :    17.50                   │
│  Items Tax   :        25.12  Tax      :     0.88  Total Tax   :       26.00 │
│                              Nominal  : 4900                       │
│                              Departmt :    0                       │
│                                                                    │
│  Items Gross :        172.32 Gross    :     5.88  Total Gross :      178.20 │
│                                                                    │
│                              Settlement Days  : 30                │
│                              Settlement Disc. :     2.50  Early Payment:  174.52 │
│                                                                    │
└──────────────────────────────────────────────────────────────────┘
```

Fig 7.4

The first three fields are **Notes** that can be placed on to the invoice. Such notes would be used to relay information to a customer.

The fields Tax Code, Nominal Code, Department and Description are only used if the entire invoice is to be posted to the Sales Ledger and Nominal Ledger as a single entity. When you entered each stock line, the details were repeated in there. There is no need to enter the details on this screen if you want the postings done individually. The only real purpose of having data in here was to demonstrate what could go in if it is to be used.

The **Carriage** figure is used if you want to charge separately for postage and packing. The carriage will need its own tax code and Nominal Code for future posting. In the final accounts, carriage charged to customers will still appear on their accounts as money owing and so is debited to the Debtors Control Account.

The settlement days shown are the number of days before payment is due and represent a facility for offering the customer some cash discount for early payment. In Fig 7.4 you will observe that the customer can have 2.5% discount if the invoice is settled within 30 days. This is then reflected in the totals on the bottom right-hand part of the screen.

When this invoice is complete, you will need to save it for future printing. Use the **Page Down** key again and you will be put back to the Header page. From here press **Esc** and you have the option of **Save**, **Edit** or **Abandon**. **Save** the invoice to add it to the file for future processing.

As a useful tip, it is often wise to batch process much of the work, in the same way as mentioned previously with respect to invoicing, credit notes and other documents. In other words, produce a large number of invoices at one time rather than on an *ad hoc* basis involving multiple visits to the computer.

Producing **Credit Notes** is identical to producing invoices. By selecting the option from the Invoice Production Menu you are given the same screen, except you see Credit Note Number instead of Invoice Number. The credit note will have the opposite effect to an invoice because it signifies a fall in the amount owing by the customer. When entering credit note details, you will thus need to be careful about which Nominal Account you post the details to.

Sage also allows a facility called **Free-Text Invoicing** which produces an invoice made up mainly of text and with only one single invoice price. The activity would prove useful if you want to make up an invoice that is not directly related to stock, for example for professional fees for a service. The only difference to invoicing from stock lies in the stock line forms. Figure 7.5 gives an example of such an invoice being made up.

```
┌─────────────────────────────────────────────────────────────────────┐
│ ┌───────────────────────────────────────────────────────────────┐   │
│ │ Accountant Plus          Free Text Invoice        18th August 199X │ │
│ └───────────────────────────────────────────────────────────────┘   │
│                                                                       │
│  Invoice No.   :      3                   Total Nett  :      68.56    │
│  Customer      : Minerva Football Co. Ltd.  Total Tax :      12.00    │
│  Item No.      :      1                    Total Gross :     80.56    │
│                                                                       │
│  Line 1        : Sundry items delivered plus repairs                  │
│  Line 2        :                                                      │
│  Line 3        :                                                      │
│  Line 4        :                                                      │
│  Line 5        :                                                      │
│  Line 6        :                                                      │
│  Line 7        :                                                      │
│  Line 8        :                                                      │
│  Line 9        :                                                      │
│                                                                       │
│  Price         :     68.56                                            │
│  Tax Code      : T1                        Nett    :        68.56     │
│  Tax Value %   :       17.50              Tax     :        12.00      │
│  Nominal Code  : 4001                                                 │
│  Department    : 0                         TOTAL   :        80.56     │
└─────────────────────────────────────────────────────────────────────┘
```

Fig 7.5

You are given nine lines in which to write whatever text you want, and are then required to enter *one* Nett price only. The VAT is calculated, depending on the tax code used. You will also need to state the Nominal Code for future posting. You should remember that this option will not ultimately affect stock levels.

Once all the invoices have been produced, it is always a good idea to extract a list of the invoices that are now stored on the system. This activity can be achieved by selecting **Display Index** from the Invoice Production menu. Figure 7.6 shows an index of invoices and you can see from this that the absence of any information in the Printed and Posted columns indicates that nothing has either been posted or printed.

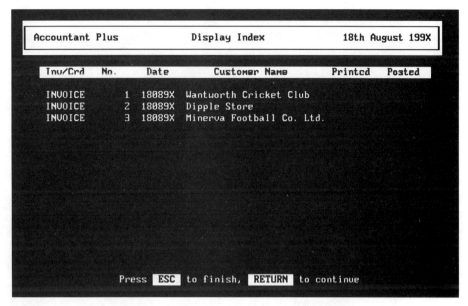

Accountant Plus		Display Index		18th August 199X

Inv/Crd	No.	Date	Customer Name	Printed	Posted
INVOICE	1	18089X	Wantworth Cricket Club		
INVOICE	2	18089X	Dipple Store		
INVOICE	3	18089X	Minerva Football Co. Ltd.		

Press **ESC** to finish, **RETURN** to continue

Fig 7.6

PRINTING INVOICES

You can go on adding invoices at any time you want. The printing of these invoices is then done separately at a later stage. This has the advantage of saving considerable time in setting up your printer for each invoice. You can for example, enter invoice details many times in a week but allocate only one time in the week to print them. The strategy should be to enter batches of invoices fairly regularly in order to keep the stock files updated and the Sales and Nominal Ledger well posted.

Your first step will be to prepare the format of the invoice so that it can be printed in a form suitable to your business. This can be a time-consuming and awkward job but it normally needs doing only once. To help you, Sage sells preprinted stationery with a layout exactly tailored to the way the invoices have been set up when the package is purchased and installed.

Whether you are using Sage-produced stationery or your own, you will still have to make some changes to the stationery layout. From the main **Utilities** menu select **Stationery Layout**. You will need to alter two documents, Invoices (Stock) and Invoices (Free Format). Select the **Invoices (Stock)** first. The computer will now ask you to enter the name of the file that stores the letter. The file shown is INVOICE.LYT and this is the file that stores the layout of the invoices. Press **Enter** (**Return**) to select this and you will see the file that is used to print invoices to customers.

Now use the arrow keys to move around the invoice. If you want to delete any text then use the **Delete** or **Del** key to do it. Text can be inserted by typing in what you want. Figure 7.7 shows the top half of the invoice, which has had some of its text altered to suit a different company. It also shows that text has been added to give some more meaning to the figures. The invoice assumes Sage stationery is being used which has much of the text already preprinted. You can also order stationery from Sage with your business name and logo already printed on it.

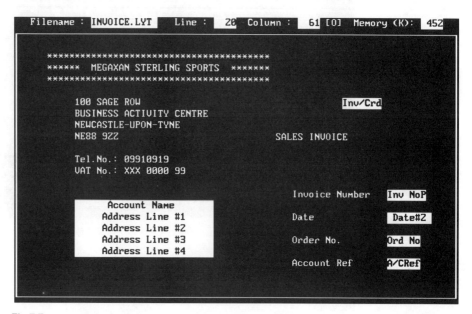

Fig 7.7

The text highlighted with a white background indicates the positioning of field data extracted from the data in the Sales Ledger files. When the invoices are printed, the field data will appear on the invoice where indicated. You can delete any of these fields using the **Del** key. Function key F4 displays on the right-hand side of the screen the available fields that can be inserted into the invoice.

When you have made the necessary changes, press the **Esc** key. Saving the changes will have the effect of making the changes permanent. If you feel you have made too many errors, then you can always choose the Abandon option and start again.

You can examine the changes when you print an invoice. If you are using your own independent stationery then a good deal of time may have to be spent putting everything in the right place.

Just as you changed the invoice for invoicing from stock, you will also have to do the same for free format invoices. Again from the main **Utilities** menu, select **Stationery Layout** and from here **Invoices (Free Format)**. The file that stores details about this document is INVTEXT.LYT and you can see an example of part of it being edited in Fig 7.8.

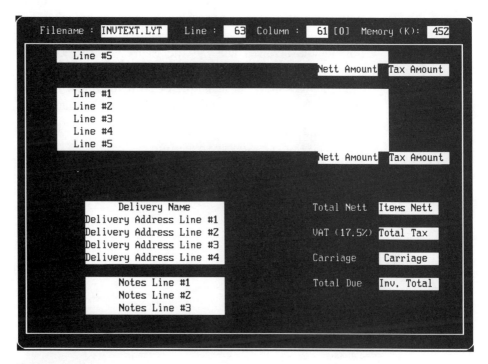

Fig 7.8

Once this has been done, the next step is to try to print invoices to see if they are as required. From the Invoice Production menu in the Sales Ledger select **Print Invoice**. You will first be asked to state the range of invoices you want printed from invoice number to invoice number. If you want all of them printed, just accept the values offered to you. Input file name will be shown as INVOICE.LYT. This can be changed if you have a different file where the invoice details are stored.

The next question asks if you want to ignore printed flags. If you answer **N**(o) to this, then all invoices previously printed will *not* be printed again. If you answer **Y**(es), then *all* invoices in the selected range will be printed, irrespective of whether they have been printed before.

You will next be given the opportunity of either sending the invoices direct to the printer or to a named file for future processing. The final question asks if you want to pause between each printed invoice. If you answer **Y**(es) to this, the computer will stop printing at the end of each invoice and prompt you when you are ready for the next one.

Print some invoices to see the effect of your work. If the invoices have not come out as hoped, then you can return to utilities and amend the stationery layout. Then return to the print invoice option, remembering to ask the computer to print again those invoices already printed (answer **Y** at ignore printed flag prompt).

The free text invoices will also print with the invoices from stock. When printing all invoices, the free text invoices will print on the same stationery, unless you have changed it during the printing process.

While invoices are printing, Sage sends the information back to the file holding the invoices and the file is updated to record which invoices have been printed.

Figure 7.9 shows an example of an invoice that has been printed after the changes were made through the stationery layouts facility.

```
****************************************************
****** MEGAXAN STERLING SPORTS ******
****************************************************
```

100 SAGE ROW   Invoice
BUSINESS ACTIVITY CENTRE
NEWCASTLE-UPON-TYNE
NE88 9ZZ

SALES INVOICE

Tel No: 09910919
VAT No: XXX 0000 99

Invoice Number: 4

Sports Super Centre
Sports Arena   Date: 19/08/9X
London
                                  Order No: 332
                                  Account Ref: 0050

QUANTITY	DETAILS	DISC	NETT PRICE	VAT
5.00	Tennis Play Kit	5.00	237.50	40.94
3.00	T-Shirt – Medium Red/White	10.00	34.96	6.03
2.00	T-Shirts Small Red/White	10.00	22.50	3.88
2.00	T-Shirts Large Red/White	10.00	24.80	4.27
20.00	Tennis Balls	10.00	21.60	3.72

Delivery Address

------ AS INVOICED ------   Total Nett Price   341.36

                                          VAT (17.5%)   60.59

                                          Carriage   10.00

Please phone for details   Total Due   411.95
about our special offers

Fig 7.9

UPDATING THE LEDGERS

Until now the Sales Ledger and Stock Control have not been informed of the invoices and credit notes that have been produced. Soon after you have

MEGAXAN STERLING SPORTS Invoice Production – Update Ledgers Date: 18C89X Page: 1

Inv/Credit	Number	Date	A/C	No	N/C	Dep	Stock Code	Stock Description	Quantity	Nett Amount	Tc	Tax Amount

Invoice No 1 has not been POSTED due to:
Insufficient STOCK levels

Inv/Credit	Number	Date	A/C	No	N/C	Dep	Stock Code	Stock Description	Quantity	Nett Amount	Tc	Tax Amount
Invoice No	2	18089X	0040	115	4002	0	ALL			199.73	T1	34.95
Invoice No	3	18089X	0070	116	4001	0		Sundry items delivered		68.56	T1	12.00

Fig 7.10

entered the invoice details, it is a wise policy to update the ledgers in order to keep the accounts up to date.

Select the **Update Ledgers** activity from the Invoice Production menu. You will be asked for the range of invoices to post. If you want all of them posted, press **Enter** (Return) to both suggested amounts. Figure 7.10 is a report showing three invoices being posted.

You will observe that the first invoice was not posted because there was insufficient stock. If, for some other reason, the posting cannot be done, then the appropriate error message will come up.

While the postings are being done, the file that holds the invoices will be updated to show which invoices have been posted. This will be used by Sage to ensure that a situation never arises where an invoice is posted twice.

At this stage there are a number of reports within Stock Control that will show you the effect the invoicing has had on stock. Figure 7.11 shows the Stock Profit Reports as a result of some invoicing.

MEGAXAN STERLING SPORTS Stock Profit Reports – Month to Date

Category : 1 : Sports Clothing

Stock Code	Description	Quantity Sold	Sales Value	Cost Of Sales	Profit	Profit (%)
00010	T-Shirts Medium Red/White	10.00	113.31	90.00	23.31	25.90
00020	T-Shirts Small Red/White	6.00	65.62	54.00	11.62	21.52
00030	T-Shirts Large Red/White	1.00	12.06	8.00	4.06	50.75
00040	Scarves	1.00	8.74	4.00	4.74	118.50
		Totals :	199.73	156.00	43.73	28.03

Fig 7.11

Other reports worth examining are within the Sales Ledger function. From **Day Books** in the Sales Ledger you can select **Invoices** to get a listing of all the invoices sent out via the Invoice Production activities.

Figure 7.12 is an example of a transactions history with a customer. The report was extracted using **Transaction History** from the Sales Ledger main menu.

Figure 7.12 shows all the individual item lines sent in Invoice 4.

If you want to start either your invoice numbers or credit note numbers at a number higher than 1, then you can do so by entering a different invoice or credit note number when preparing it. Any number selected will cause Sage to add 1 to the next invoice number as default.

MONTH END

One of the problems you are going to find is that files will start to get too large as the year progresses. A policy often adopted by businesses is to

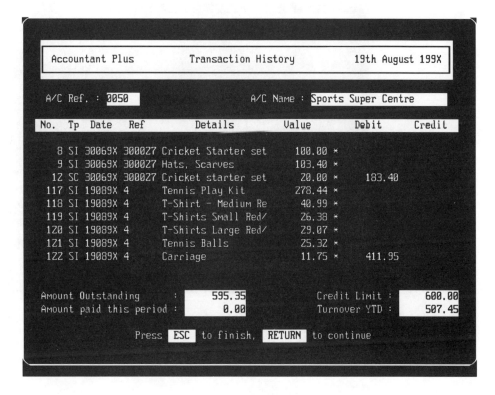

```
┌──────────────────────────────────────────────────────────────────┐
│  ┌──────────────────────────────────────────────────────────┐    │
│  │ Accountant Plus      Transaction History    19th August 199X │  │
│  └──────────────────────────────────────────────────────────┘    │
│                                                                    │
│   A/C Ref. : 0050              A/C Name : Sports Super Centre       │
│                                                                    │
│   No.  Tp  Date    Ref      Details        Value     Debit   Credit │
│                                                                    │
│     8  SI 30069X 300027 Cricket Starter set  100.00 ×             │
│     9  SI 30069X 300027 Hats, Scarves        103.40 ×             │
│    12  SC 30069X 300027 Cricket starter set   20.00 ×    183.40   │
│   117  SI 19089X 4      Tennis Play Kit      278.44 ×             │
│   118  SI 19089X 4      T-Shirt - Medium Re   40.99 ×             │
│   119  SI 19089X 4      T-Shirts Small Red/   26.38 ×             │
│   120  SI 19089X 4      T-Shirts Large Red/   29.07 ×             │
│   121  SI 19089X 4      Tennis Balls          25.32 ×             │
│   122  SI 19089X 4      Carriage              11.75 ×    411.95   │
│                                                                    │
│   Amount Outstanding       :    595.35    Credit Limit :   600.00 │
│   Amount paid this period  :      0.00    Turnover YTD :   507.45 │
│                                                                    │
│          Press  ESC  to finish,  RETURN  to continue              │
└──────────────────────────────────────────────────────────────────┘
```

Fig 7.12

undergo some extra month-ending routines. You have already done some month-ending routines when handling recurring entries, Prepayments, Accruals and Depreciation. Now you should take the whole thing a stage further.

At the end of each month it is a good idea to clear away all those invoices that have been fully processed and paid. This was explained earlier and should form part of the end-of-month routine.

From the **Utilities** menu, you can select the **Month-End** activity and you get the four options. The **Stock** option will have the effect of clearing the stock histories, thus reducing the size of the stock file. It will also set all quantities sold in month and values sold in month to zero. When running this option you are told that you need three reports printed out: Stock Reference Sheet, Stock Valuation Report and Stock Profit Report.

To reduce the amount of information building up on your system, you can also run a reconfiguration routine. This will have the effect of removing *all* completed transactions from your accounts data. It can increase your disk space quite considerably, but various reports ought to extracted first. From the **Utilities** main menu you would select **Data File Utilities** and from there **Data File Changes** and then **Reconfiguration**. When you get this far, you see a screen similar to the one shown in Fig 7.13.

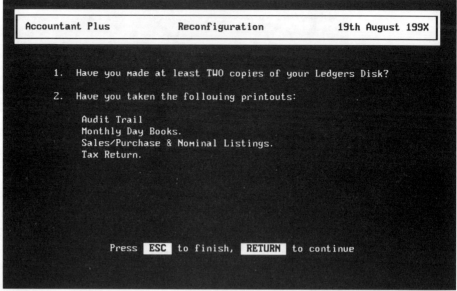

┌───┐
│ Accountant Plus   Reconfiguration   19th August 199X   │
└───┘

    1. Have you made at least TWO copies of your Ledgers Disk?

    2. Have you taken the following printouts:

        Audit Trail
        Monthly Day Books.
        Sales/Purchase & Nominal Listings.
        Tax Return.

           Press ESC to finish, RETURN to continue

Fig 7.13

You are now asked if you have made two copies of your ledger disk. These are backups which will be the only place where many transactions are held, so it is important to have them on disks in case they are needed for future reference.

The printouts are important for auditing reference purposes, and the system gives you a list of Audit Trail, Monthly Day Books, Sales/Purchases and Nominal listings, and Tax Return.

A summary of month-end routines could read:

1   Extract an Audit Trail for the month
2   Complete all transactions for the month
3   Check for errors and omissions and put them right, in particular sorting out the suspense account
4   Extract Tax Returns for the month
5   Tidy up the Nominal Ledger
6   Extract from Sales and Purchase Ledger:
      Aged Debtors Report
      Customer Statements
      Monthly Day Books
      Sales and Purchase reports
7   Extract from the Nominal Ledger statements of profit
8   Extract from Stock Control:
      Stock Reference Sheet
      Stock Valuation Report
      Stock Profit Report
9   Backup the files

10 Perform month-end routines through **utilities** for:
   Recurring entries
   Prepayments and Accruals
   Depreciation
   Stock
11 Perform reconfiguration routine

Having automated these transactions, direct entry to the Sales Ledger need only be for payments by customers and adjustments of customer accounts. These often require very little information from the operator.

CONCLUSION

By now you should have appreciated that, once the system has been set up, most of the data entry functions can be avoided. For example, because the system knows about your customers and your stock, it makes invoice production quicker with less effort. In fact, the only real data entry needed in the Sales Ledger is when a customer settles debt or you need to make alterations to a customer's record or add new customers.

In the next chapter you will see that the process can be taken one step further, with orders being processed prior to invoices being produced.

You are advised to give yourself a little more practice before moving on.

8 Sales and purchase order processing

INTRODUCTION

This final chapter on the actual accounting functions in Sage concentrates on the ordering side of business activities. Both sales and purchase ordering are available to Sage **Financial Controller** users only. This chapter will start by examining the Sales Order Processing function before going on to look at Purchase Orders.

The purpose of Sales Order Processing is to process orders placed by customers. Basically, an order is placed by a customer and processed by the business and is then completed by the despatch of the goods or carrying out of the service, accompanied by or followed by an invoice. In Purchase Order processing, on the other hand, the business sends an order for stock to a supplier. In both cases, such order processing will have an implication for stock and so relies on stock records being up to date.

SALES ORDER PROCESSING

This function will help a business to maintain efficient and adequate stock levels. When an order is received and entered into the computer, stock records are adjusted to indicate that certain stocks have been *allocated* against an order. Sales Order Processing can be broken down into distinct stages:

1   The order is received by the business from its customer. The order could now be invoiced and the goods despatched. This has the effect of reducing stock levels. The problem may arise where there is insufficient stock to meet the order.

2   The second stage is to decide whether the order could be partially met by despatching and invoicing for the goods that are available and then sending the rest of the order out when the rest of the goods become available. Although perfectly acceptable in many businesses, it is going to be important to keep a record of what has been delivered. It is a practice by many businesses that when they place an order, they do not want immediate delivery as it creates too high a stock level.

3 You may decide to hold on to an order until it can be met in full. For this to work properly, you will need to keep stock 'allocated' against an order. The purpose of doing this is to ensure that, as you wait for sufficient stock to complete the order, you do not despatch what goods you do have available to another customer.

When an order is received, a stock allocation is made to indicate that items of stock will be needed to meet the order. The stock file record, therefore, is updated to reflect this. As a consequence, when decisions have to be made about stock, a more rational decision can be made because it is known what stock is required to meet sales orders. When stocks are available to meet an order or complete an order, the stock levels have to be reduced by what has been despatched, as well as removing from stock records the allocation details. In other words, an allocation becomes an adjustment out.

When an order is received from a customer, the business may acknowledge receipt of the order by sending the customer a Sales Acknowledgement document. This document will need setting up in the same way as the invoices, credit notes and statements using the **Stationery Layout** facility from the **Utilities** function of Sage.

The Sales Order Processing function illustrated in Fig 8.1 gives you an idea of how Sage handles the Sales Orders.

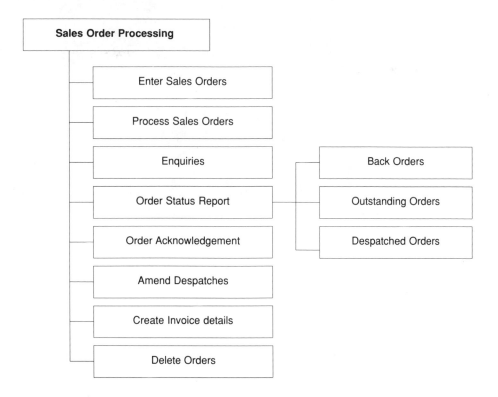

Fig 8.1

Entering orders

When an order is received it may appear on your own order form stationery or on the customer's own order form, depending on the policy of the customer. Increasingly, orders are placed by telex or by fax (facsimile telegraphy), which allows orders to be reproduced on the recipient's fax via a telephone line. Many businesses will also accept orders by telephone, with the operator entering details straight on to the computer.

Whatever method is used, the receipt of the order will be the point of **Data Capture** and it needs placing on to the computer. For most businesses, it will involve an operator entering the order on to the computer using an order form to gather the initial details.

From the Sales Order Processing function select **Enter Orders** and you will see a blank form appear on the screen looking very much like the first page of an invoice. Figure 8.2 shows the first page with customer details entered.

```
┌────────────────────────────────────────────────────────────────┐
│ Financial Controller      Enter Sales Orders        30th August 199X │
└────────────────────────────────────────────────────────────────┘

Order No.          :      1

Date               : 30089X       Order Taken By  : DR
Sales Ref.         : 0010
                                  Invoice No.         :      0
Customer Name      : Wantworth Cricket Club    Due Delivery    : 25109X
Customer Address   : The Sports Centre   Customer Order No. : 55521
     ..            : Hydean Way
     ..            : Perth             Allocation Status  :
     ..            :                   Despatch  Status   :

Telephone          : 0999-3289103
                                        Total Nett  :       88.22
Delivery Name      : ------ AS INVOICED ------    Total Tax   :    15.44
Delivery Address   :
     ..            :                   Total Gross :      103.66
     ..            :
     ..            :                   Early Payment :    103.66
```

Fig 8.2

The similarity between this and the invoice is largely to be expected because all the details that will appear on the eventual invoice will be generated from the initial order.

At this point it is worth examining the details that make up a record within the Outstanding Orders file. Each order, once entered, will be placed on to an Orders file until it is completed or cancelled. Each order entered will be represented in the file by a single record. As each order is met, an invoice is sent to the customer and the record that relates to outstanding orders will need to be amended and eventually deleted from the file.

The information you will need to complete the fields that make up a sales order record include the customer account number, which will have to appear in the Sales Ledger. When this is entered, customer details will appear on the screen. You can select the appropriate record by using function key F4 to view and select a customer account held on the Sales Ledger. The order number will be displayed as 1 greater than the previous order processed, which can be changed if you wish.

The Order Taken By field can be used by the business for any purpose. It can be used to indicate which person in the business processed the order or how the order was received, e.g. by post, telephone or fax.

The Invoice Number that appears on the right-hand side of the screen in Figure 8.2 indicates the invoice number that will be given when the order is converted to an invoice. This number is distinct from the Order Number.

The Due Delivery date is the date on which you expect to fill the order or is the date the customer expects to receive the goods. This will be important for future monitoring and decision-making regarding priorities for the allocation or despatch of stock.

The allocation and despatch status is used later by the computer to indicate how far the order has been processed. Allocation Status will show whether all the goods on this order have been fully allocated, partly allocated or not allocated at all. Exactly the same information is given in the Despatch Status about whether the goods have been completely despatched, partly despatched or not despatched at all.

Once this page has been completed, pressing the **Page Down** key allows you to enter the product lines that have been ordered; a page is required for each line ordered. Figure 8.3 illustrates such a product line where this customer has ordered three scarves.

```
┌──────────────────────────────────────────────────────────────────────┐
│  Financial Controller        Enter Sales Orders         30th August 199X │
└──────────────────────────────────────────────────────────────────────┘

Order No.     :      1                    Total Nett   :      80.23
Customer      : Wantworth Cricket Club    Total Tax    :      14.04
Item No.      :      2                    Total Gross  :      94.27

Stock Code    : 00040                     Allocation Status :
Description   : scarves                    Despatch  Status :
Comment 1     :
   ..    2    :                           Qty Allocated    :       0.00
                                          Qty Despatched   :       0.00
Quantity      :      3.00
                              Exceeds Current Stock levels :       1.00
Units         : 1            Available Stock to make up    :       0.00
Unit Price    :      9.99
                                          Cost       :      29.97
Discount %    :     20.00                 Discount   :       5.99
Tax Code      : T1                        Subtotal   :      23.98
Tax Value %   :     17.50                 Tax        :       4.20
Nominal Code  : 4000
Department    : 0                         TOTAL      :      28.18
```

Fig 8.3

Again, the details are the same as those entered on an invoice, where the product is identified and the quantity and price details entered. On each page you will see on the right side the allocation and despatch status for that product line only.

Also, you will observe that the screen will show if any stock has been allocated for the order or despatched to the customer. If none has been allocated then the stock, if there is any, is available for purchase by another customer. You should not attempt to place numbers in these fields now as a later activity will allow you to allocate or despatch goods.

If there is insufficient stock to meet an order, you will see a prompt on the screen indicating this. Also, you will be prompted if a customer orders goods that would result in their credit limit being exceeded.

When you have completed the detail lines for each stock type, a final screen will be displayed for you to enter details such as carriage and discounts, which will be needed when an invoice is produced.

Once the order is complete and saved, you will enter the details into an Orders File which will have no affect on either the stock records or customer accounts in the Sales Ledger. Consequently, any errors or omissions can be put right without an affect on the accounts. As with invoicing, there is a lot of sense in batch processing the activity of entering orders rather than doing these one at a time.

Processing sales orders

Before going any further, an explanation is required of the different kinds of order referred to by Sage.

A **back order** refers to an order that has only been placed on to the system and has no stock allocated to it. This may be because of insufficient stock to meet it or because the business is holding back on further processing due to a customer exceeding their credit limit. Alternatively, it may simply be because the order has only just been placed into the file.

An **outstanding order** refers to an order that has had stock allocated to it but has not yet been despatched. In many cases, part of an outstanding order may have been despatched with the remainder of the order awaiting further stock. The situation then arises where such orders have been processed but not completed.

A **completed order** is one where all the goods that have been ordered have been despatched. In this instance, you can remove such details as they are no longer needed except for reporting or information purposes.

Processing a sales order, therefore, goes through all back orders and allocates stock to them. It will also go through outstanding orders to see if they can be completed by allocating stock, where possible, to the rest of the order.

Accessing this is done from the Sales Order Processing menu using the **Process Sales Orders** activity option. The screen shows the first twelve orders and allows you to go through each order manually, deciding whether to allocate stock or to allow the computer to do it for you automatically. Figure 8.4 illustrates such a screen.

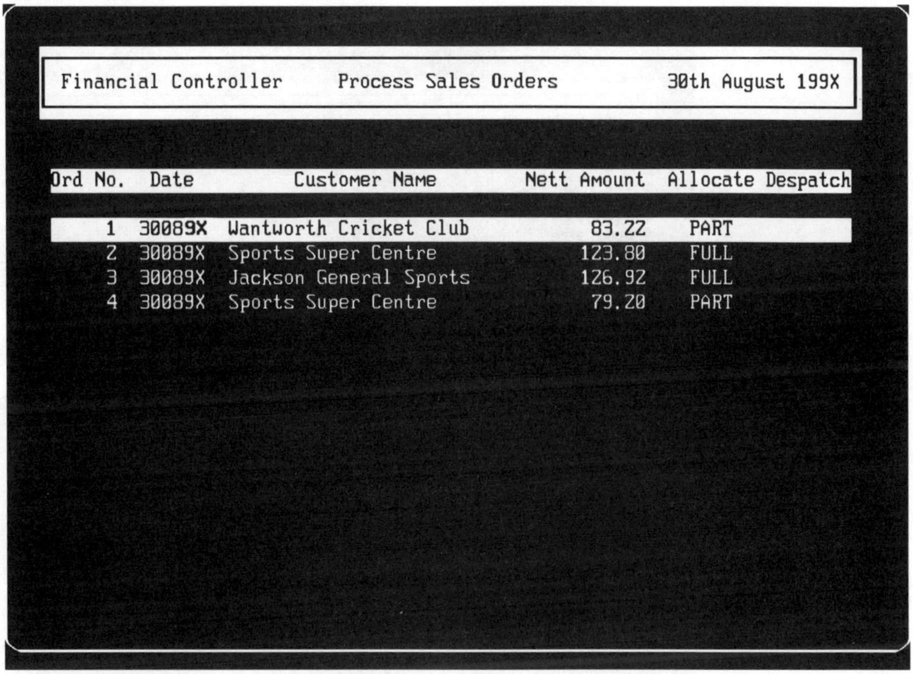

```
┌──────────────────────────────────────────────────────────────────────┐
│ Financial Controller      Process Sales Orders      30th August 199X   │
└──────────────────────────────────────────────────────────────────────┘

Ord No.  Date       Customer Name          Nett Amount  Allocate Despatch

     1   30089X  Wantworth Cricket Club         83.22   PART
     2   30089X  Sports Super Centre           123.80   FULL
     3   30089X  Jackson General Sports        126.92   FULL
     4   30089X  Sports Super Centre            79.20   PART
```

Fig 8.4

When you use **automatic**, the system will ask if you want to despatch or allocate the goods. If you choose to allocate the goods, then the stock record is updated indicating the goods are allocated to an order and such stock will then be held for the order. If you decide to choose **despatch**, then all goods that can be despatched will be removed from the stock quantities rather than simply allocated.

The despatch process searches through each product line and converts the amounts allocated as despatched. This can also be achieved by creating invoices from the orders and this will be covered later.

Figure 8.5 shows the overall effect on the stock orders where two orders are now completely allocated. In other words, the goods have been allocated and the complete order can be despatched.

If you select manual processing rather than automatic, you will go through each line of stock deciding on the status required. Apart from allocating or despatching stock, there are other options. If you choose **Unallocate** you simply take away the amounts already allocated; this may be necessary if you want to free stock and complete another order. You can also **cancel** an order, which will reverse the allocation and despatch processes and remove the order from all future reports. There is also the option of **Hold Credit** which has the effect of keeping the invoice on file but not doing anything with it until the order is subsequently allocated.

```
┌─────────────────────────────────────────────────────────────────────┐
│  ┌─────────────────────────────────────────────────────────────────┐ │
│  │ Financial Controller      Amend Despatches        30th August 199X│ │
│  └─────────────────────────────────────────────────────────────────┘ │
│                                                                       │
│   Order No. :      3          Customer Name : Jackson General Sports  │
│   A/C Ref.  : 0020                Notes  1  :                         │
│   Date      : 30089X                  ..   2  :                       │
│   Del Date  : 25089X   Item No. :  1  ..   3  :                       │
│  ┌──────────────────────────────────────────────────────────────────┐│
│   Stock Code      Stock Description   Nett Amount Quantity Allocate Despatch│
│  ├──────────────────────────────────────────────────────────────────┤│
│   00010            T-Shirt - Medium Red      64.75    5.00    5.00    5.00 │
│   00020            T-Shirts Small Red/W      62.50    5.00    5.00    5.00 │
│   00030            T-Shirts Large Red/W      13.78    1.00    1.00    1.00 │
│                                                                       │
└─────────────────────────────────────────────────────────────────────┘
```

Fig 8.5

Creating invoices

From the Sales Order Processing menu you can select the option **Create Invoices**. This passes all orders to the Sales Ledger as invoices, providing the orders are allocated in full or part. Figure 8.6 illustrates the report that will be given. Each order is given an invoice number as determined in the Sales Ledger and an invoice is created for it. In addition to the invoice details being made up, the Sales Ledger accounts will also be updated with the invoice details.

MEGAXAN STERLING SPORTS

Sales Orders – Create Invoice Details

Order	Date	A/C	Customer Name	Inv.No
1	30089x	0010	Wantworth Cricket Club	5
2	30089x	0050	Sports Super Centre	6
3	30089x	0020	Jackson General Sports	7
4	30089x	0050	Sports Super Centre	8

Fig 8.6

The end result of this is that the details about goods sent to a customer need only be entered once. This is a principle of good computerised practice where there is no need, having put details on to the computer, to have to enter such details again.

When you are ready to despatch the goods, the invoice can be printed in the usual way and the orders processed to update the stock file.

Order enquiries

From the **Enquiries** option of the Sales Order Processing menu, you can observe a fairly detailed report of the orders that are on file. Figure 8.7 is an example of such a record in the report.

MEGAXAN STERLING SPORTS   Sales Orders – Enquiries

Order No   :   122 Customer Name : Wantworth Cricket Club   Allocation Status :   Order Value : 83.22
Order Date : 30089x   A/C Reference   : 0010   Despatch Status : PART

Stock Code	Stock Description	Ordered Quantity	Allocate Quantity	Despatch Quantity	Allocate Status	Despatch Status	Despatch Date
00020	T-Shirts Small Red/White	5.00	0.00	5.00		COMPLETE	31089x
00040	Scarves	3.00	0.00	1.00		PART	31089x

Fig 8.7

From this example you can see what has been ordered and the fact that the order has been partially despatched. You will also see that the allocated status field indicates that nothing has been allocated. This could be due to the fact that there are no scarves in stock to allocate to this order or that what stock there is has been allocated to another order.

Status reports

The Sales Order Processing function allows three status reports on orders. From the **Order Status** report option you can extract details about **back**

orders. These details are for all those orders that cannot be processed because there is either insufficient stock to meet them or they are being held for credit reasons. The **Outstanding orders** report will reveal details about orders that can be partly or fully completed. The **Despatched orders** report will give details about orders that have been despatched.

When all three reports are available, a decision can be made to unallocate stock for one partially completed order so that you are able to complete another. Many of these decisions have to be taken by the business rather than the computer because there are often external circumstances that have to be taken into account.

Order acknowledgements

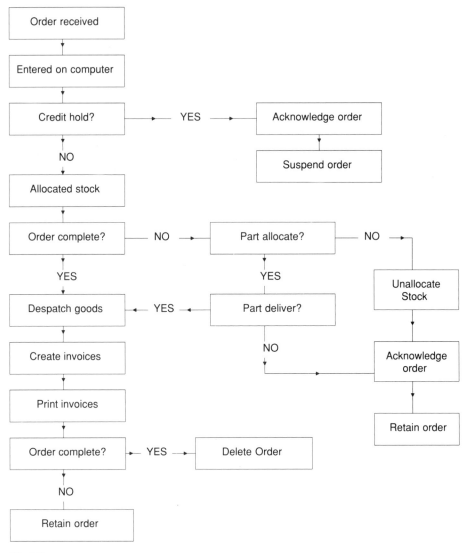

Fig 8.8

An order acknowledgment is a document sent to a customer to acknowledge an order received. Such documents are used by businesses that cannot or do not as normal practice despatch goods as soon as an order is received.

The option is available in the Sales Order Processing menu as **Order Acknowledgement** and prints the documents in exactly the same way as it prints an invoice. The file where the acknowledgement details are stored is SAORDER.LYT and should be altered to suit the business, or another one created. It can be altered in the same way as invoices by using the **Stationery Layout** option from the **Utilities** menu.

Order acknowledgements are useful to a customer to confirm the details of an order as well as to give due dates when goods are expected to arrive. Figure 8.8 shows the procedures through which an order may go when processed. You can observe from this that it is not always necessary for an acknowledgment order to be sent.

Delete orders

Deleting orders helps keeps the size of the files small and speed up many of the activities. You will only be able to delete completed orders. If an order needs to be cancelled which has been part delivered, then you should first cancel the order before trying to delete it.

Exercises on sales order processing

As a conclusion to Sales Order Processing, try the following exercises.

1 Amend the Order Acknowledgement document using the Stationery Layout activity within the Utilities function.
2 Process a number of sales orders by entering imaginary orders placed by customers for goods or services.
3 Cancel and amend one or two of these orders.
4 Allocate stock, where available, to these orders.
5 Despatch stock for these orders.
6 Create invoices from the orders and go to the Sales Ledger and update the customers' records.
7 Delete the completed orders.
8 Investigate the effect these activities have had on the stock records, Sales Ledger accounts and the Nominal Ledger accounts.

PURCHASE ORDER PROCESSING

By now you should have a good idea of the operation of the Stock Control function and the activities involved in maintaining stock records, entering stock movements and extracting reports. The final stage is to cover Purchase Order Processing, which will make use of both the Purchase Ledger and Stock Control functions. In addition to issuing orders, this function will have an effect on the stock available to be issued and, when a receipt of stock has been recorded against a purchase, will affect the physical stock quantity held.

When ordering goods, a Purchase Order will be issued and sent to a supplier. In some cases, you may have to send orders to certain suppliers on their own purchase order forms. Whatever way a Purchase Order is sent, a record must be made and details of the amounts ordered must be stored in the stock records. Each stock record will contain details of what is on order so that any reference to a stock record will give you a picture of the stock situation. When stock levels are low, it is important to know whether any more is on order, if only to avoid ordering stock more than once.

In addition to keeping stock records updated with what is on order, a Purchase Order file will also need to be kept so that you are able to keep track of orders placed and report on those orders that are late in being met by suppliers. There will be a record held in the file for each Purchase Order still outstanding.

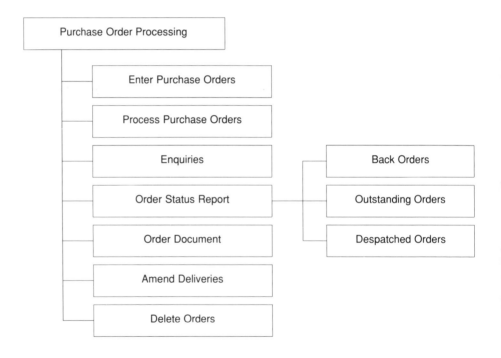

Fig 8.9

Figure 8.9 shows the structure of the Purchase Order Processing function and you will find that it differs very little from Sales Order Processing. Consequently, not much will need to be explained in this chapter regarding the operation of Purchase Order Processing. The processes involved are, however, more straightforward as the onus of getting the goods to their destination in time falls on the supplier.

To enter a Purchase Order is the same process as for a Sales Order. Figure 8.10 shows an example of the first page being entered.

```
┌────────────────────────────────────────────────────────────────────────┐
│                                                                          │
│   ┌───────────────────────────────────────────────────────────────┐     │
│   │  Financial Controller    Enter Purchase Orders      30th August 199X │
│   └───────────────────────────────────────────────────────────────┘     │
│                                                                          │
│                                                                          │
│      Order No.          :      1                                         │
│                                                                          │
│      Date               : 30089X      Order Placed By  : Jane            │
│      Purchase Ref.      : P0010                                          │
│                                                                          │
│      Supplier Name      : Ideal Sportswear plc    Due Despatch    : 25109X │
│      Supplier Address   : 120 Spring Gardens                             │
│         ..              : Hillingsworth                                  │
│         ..              : Northampton             Order   Status  :      │
│         ..              : NN2Z                    Delivery Status :      │
│                                                                          │
│      Telephone          : 293912                                         │
│                                                     Total Nett  :   0.00 │
│      Despatch Name      : ------ AS ORDERED -------  Total Tax   :   0.00 │
│      Despatch Address   :                                                │
│         ..              :                           Total Gross :   0.00 │
│         ..              :                                                │
│         ..              :                           Early Payment :   0.00 │
│                                                                          │
└────────────────────────────────────────────────────────────────────────┘
```

Fig 8.10

The Order Number is again generated by the computer and the purchase reference is extracted from the Purchase Ledger. The Due Despatch date is the date when you want or expect the goods to be despatched to you. Some of the terms are often agreed with the supplier beforehand and can be entered to confirm the arrangements.

The rest of the order is made up in exactly the same way as for a Sales Order and is also stored in a file. Once orders have been placed on to the file they should then be processed. The effect of processing is to update the stock records with what is on order. Figure 8.11 shows an example of a purchase order being processed.

First you are asked if you want to process the orders manually or automatically. If you choose **automatic** you will be asked if you are simply updating the stock records with what is **on order** or entering the orders as **delivered**, in which case the stock quantities are increased by the amounts that have been delivered. If you select **manual**, then there are just four kinds of purchase order status you can enter: **On-Order**, **Cancelled**, **Part Delivered** or **Complete**.

```
┌──────────────────────────────────────────────────────────────────┐
│                                                                    │
│   ┌──────────────────────────────────────────────────────────┐    │
│   │ Financial Controller    Process Purchase Orders    30th August 199x │
│   └──────────────────────────────────────────────────────────┘    │
│                                                                    │
│   ─────────────────────────────────────────────────────────────  │
│   Ord No.  Date        Supplier Name        Nett Amount  On-Order Delivery │
│                                                                    │
│         1  30089X  Ideal Sportswear plc         63.00            │
│                                                                    │
│                                                                    │
│                                                                    │
│                                                                    │
│                                                                    │
│                                                                    │
│                                                                    │
│   Do you want to : Order Delivery                                 │
│                                                                    │
└──────────────────────────────────────────────────────────────────┘
```

Fig 8.11

Order status reports work in the same way as they did for the Sales Order Processing in that you get the options on reports for **back orders**, **outstanding orders** and **despatched orders**. Figure 8.12 shows an extract from a despatched status report, showing the orders that have been delivered by suppliers.

The **Order Document** activity prints the orders for sending to suppliers. You will be asked for the file where the order documents are detailed in the same way as for printing invoices. These details are stored in a file named POORDER.LYT and can be altered to suit the business through the **Stationery Layouts** activity of the Utilities function.

An option that does not exist with the Purchase Order Processing is the creation of invoices. Purchasing does not require a business to generate an invoice because the supplier will be sending their invoice with the goods. The result of this is that updating the Purchase Ledger cannot be done automatically. Instead, when an invoice is received, you will have to update the Purchase Ledger by going through the Purchase Ledger function as you did before.

When you examine stock records, you will now get a complete picture as the stock record will show what is in stock, what stock has been allocated to an order and what stock is actually on order with suppliers. With such a complete picture, it now becomes far easier to keep a close check on stock and maintain a better degree of efficiency.

MEGAXAN STERLING SPORTS   Order Status Reports – Delivered Orders

Order No.   :   1   Supplier Ref.   : P0010   Supplier Number   :
Order Date   : 30089x   Supplier Name   : Ideal Sportswear plc Despatch Name   : ----AS ORDERED ----
                                Supplier Address : 120 Spring Gardens   Despatch Address :
Notes   :   : Hillingsworth   :
             :   : Northampton   :
             :   : NN22   :

Placed By   : Jane   Telephone Number : 293912   Despatch Date   : 25109x

Stock Code   Stock Description   Comment 1   Comment 2   Quantity   Dis't   Price

00010   T-Shirt – Medium Red/White   10.00   30.00   63.00

                                              Carriage :   0.00   Order Total :   63.00

==

Orders Total Value :   63.00

Fig 8.12

Exercises on purchase order processing

As a conclusion to this chapter, try the following exercises.

1   Amend the Purchase Order Document using the Stationery Layout activity within the Utilities function.
2   Process a number of purchase orders by entering imaginary details of orders placed with suppliers for goods or services.
3   Cancel and amend one or two of these orders.
4   Update the stock records to show that goods are on order.
5   Enter some orders as delivered.
6   Go into the Purchase Ledger and update the Purchase Ledger with invoices received. You should extract a report similar to that set out in Fig 8.12 to assist you.
7   Delete the completed orders.
8   Investigate the effect these activities have had on the stock records.

9 Advanced Sage utilities

INTRODUCTION

Throughout the duration of this book, a good deal of the practical effort has been in the extraction of a whole series of reports. Often, however, information in the existing reports available with the package is not in the format required. Report Generation is, in effect, an extra way of extracting reports from the system. The difference lies in the fact that it is up to you what reports you want and the format in which you want them. Using this facility is rather like programming the computer yourself – you determine the rules and the output.

In addition to being able to print reports, you may want to incorporate a report in a document of another kind that is to be generated by a word processor or a desktop publishing package. Later in this chapter, you will see how this can be achieved.

This chapter also covers details about the files that Sage generates and uses and how to manipulate them and back up and restore them.

REPORT GENERATOR

From **Utilities** select the **Report Generator** function. This will reveal the following menu:

Sales Ledger
Purchase Ledger
Nominal Ledger
Management Reports
Invoice Production
Stock Control
Sales Order Processing
Purchase Order Processing

The number of the options available to you for generating reports will depend on the level of Sage you use – this menu is for Financial Controller. From this menu select **Sales Ledger** and you will be presented with a list of reports already generated and stored on your disk when you installed Sage. You can at this stage select one of the existing reports or create a new one yourself. For most businesses the existing reports are quite adequate for their needs, along with the other reports available from within the ledgers.

From the list of reports, highlight the one with the title **Sales Ledger Reports – Turnover Month & YTD** and press the **Enter** (Return) key. The program now asks if you want to Run, Edit or Delete the report. Select **Edit** by highlighting the option and press the **Enter** key again.

You will first be given the opportunity to alter the title of the report. This title should indicate the subject of the report, as it will appear on the report. If you do not want the title altered, press the **Enter** key again and a screen similar to the one shown in Fig 9.1 will appear.

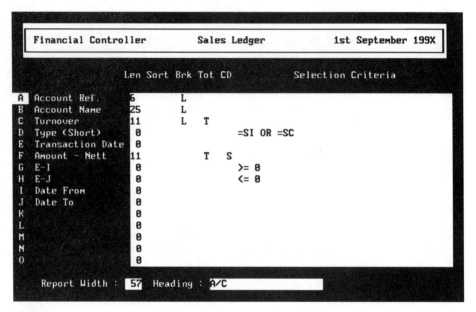

Fig 9.1

The first column in Fig 9.1 shows a list of field names that make up the report with letters beside them running from 'A' to 'O'. These field names are those that are contained in the Sales Ledger data files and were chosen to compile the report. The fields 'G' and 'H' shown in Fig 9.1 are calculated fields where G is calculated as the value in E (transaction date) minus the value in I (Date from). The highlighted area has details about the field length used on the report. Those fields with a zero in them indicate that, although the field details are used to compile the report, they will not appear on the report. From the report shown, only four fields are to appear on the printed version.

The **Sort** column is used if you want the report to sort by that particular field. If for example B had 1A in it, then the report would sort the records by Account Name first (hence '1') and in Ascending order (hence 'A'). If another field had, say, 2D in it then all the Account Names that were the same would be further sorted into **D**escending order.

The 'L' in the Brk column indicates a line break each time the field value or name changes. The 'T' in the total column instructs the program to put totals at the end of the report (and on each page if the report runs into more than one page) and also sub-totals where there might be a break. A 'Y' in this column would only put totals at the end of pages and the report.

The 'S' in the CD column indicates the Balance is to be displayed. If 'C' was entered then only Credit values would appear, while 'D' would give only Debit values.

The selection criteria decide what records are used to compile the report. On D row you will see **=SI OR =SC** which states that only Sales Invoices and Sales Credits are to be included. In row G the criteria **>= 0** means the value has to be greater or equal to zero to be included in the report. Row H has **<= 0** meaning that the value has to be less than or equal to zero to be included in the report. A criteria section requires knowledge about the field types that are stored in the file, full details of which can be found in the Sage *System Manager* manual. Also in the criteria section you can place 'Equality Operators' with 'Logical Operators', which are listed for you in Fig 9.2.

Equality Operators		Logical Operators	
=	Equal to	AND	Both conditions must be true
!=	Not equal to	OR	One condition must be true
<	Less than		
<=	Less than or Equal to		
>	Greater than		
>=	Greater than or Equal to		

Fig 9.2

Pressing the **Esc** key allows you to abandon the report and leave it unchanged. When you select the report again from the list of reports available, you can then print it. Figure 9.3 shows the kind of report that is printed from the report settings examined in Fig 9.1.

When printing a report, one of the options allows you to output the report to a file as 'Comma Separated Value Output'. This allows you to link the Sage package with a spreadsheet, database or word processor; a topic for later discussion in this chapter.

If you want to generate your own reports, then all you need to do is to enter a new report name when selecting a report and give it a new title. Selecting the field names that are used in the report can be done by pressing the function key **F4**. If you want a calculated field, the option is available

MEGAXAN STERLING SPORTS

Sales Ledger Reports – Turnover Month & YTD

A/C	Account Name	Turnover YTD	Turnover MTH
-------	------------------------------------	-------------	-------------
0020	Jackson General Sports	240.00	395.00
0030	Harriers Football Club	468.09	468.09
0040	Dipple Store	519.73	519.73
0050	Sports Super Centre	507.45	507.45
0060	Howes Gym Centre	340.00	340.00
0070	Minerva Football Co. Ltd.	478.56	68.56
		2553.83	2298.83

Fig 9.3

from the list of fields. It would be wise, however, to examine some of the reports that come with the package in order to get a good understanding of constructing reports.

Linking reports with spreadsheets

A spreadsheet is the electronic equivalent of an accountant's ledger – a large piece of paper divided by vertical columns and horizontal rows into a grid of **cells**. The name derives from **spread**ing the organisation's accounts on a **sheet** of paper, and the user can enter numbers, formulae or text into the cells. Each cell is referred to by its co-ordinates, like a map reference or point on a graph. For example, cell C12 is in column C, row 12. Formulae can be entered to link cells. An example of linking cells is where a cell entry reads:

B1 * C1

This makes the value of the contents of that cell equal to the value of cell B1 multiplied by the value of cell C1. The spreadsheet effectively becomes a screen-based calculator capable of being printed or displayed as a graph.

Any figure can be changed at any time and the new results will automatically be shown; this is called **what if** analysis (for example what if sales were to increase by 10%). It is this facility of being able quickly to recalculate formulae that makes spreadsheets a powerful, useful and popular analytical tool.

Some spreadsheets are used in order to seek goals. For example, spreadsheets can be set up to depict the sales and costs of a business. A model is set up to determine at what price profits will be maximised.

Some examples of uses are:

• Financial plans and budgets can be represented as a table, with columns for time periods (e.g. months) and rows for different elements of the plan (e.g. costs and revenue).

- Tax, investment and loan calculations.

- Statistics such as averages, standard deviations, time series and regression analysis. Many in-built statistical functions are available in the Lotus 1-2-3 software program but can be input from Sage (see below).

- Consolidation – merging branch or departmental accounts to form group (consolidated) accounts. This involves merging two or more spreadsheets together.

- Currency conversion – useful for an organisation with overseas interests such as a multinational company.

- Timetabling and roster planning of staff within organisations or departments.

Sage has the facility of outputting any file to the disk in a way that a spread-sheet program, such as Lotus 1-2-3, Multiplan or Quattro, can read in and manipulate data.

When you are about to run a report, you are given the option of sending data to a file and then asked if you want to send it to a **comma separated value output** file. If you answer **Y**(es) to this, the file created looks something like that in Fig 9.4, which was generated from the Stock Control report generator to give a price list of goods in stock.

Such files have no headings, sub-totals or totals. They are, however, in exactly the form that spreadsheets can import from. In order to import such a file you will need to refer to your spreadsheet package. To practise any of these extra facilities available through the report generator, you will need a package such as Lotus and a knowledge of the package you are trying to link with, an area of activity beyond the scope of this book.

Linking reports with other applications

Apart from the link with spreadsheets, Sage files can also link with database and word processing packages.

Database packages allow you to manipulate data as records and fields. A package such as dBase or DataEase offers a very flexible way of data storage, enquiry and reporting. You should note, however, that Sage is a form of database that has been tailored to the functions of accounting.

To incorporate Sage data into a database package, you need to output the report data to a **comma separated value file** in the same way as you did for the spreadsheet. From here, you will need to consult your database application manuals to see how to import data into the database package.

1,"Sports Clothing	","00010	""T-Shirt – Medium Red/White	""1	12.95,	10.00,	15.00,	20.00
1,"Sports Clothing	","00020	""T-Shirts Small Red/White	""1	12.50,	10.00,	15.00,	20.00
1,"Sports Clothing	","00030	""T-Shirts Large Red/White	""1	13.78,	10.00,	15.00,	20.00
1,"Sports Clothing	","00040	","Scarves	""1	9.99,	10.00,	15.00,	20.00
2,"Cricket Supplies	","00050	""Cricket Pads	""Pair	15.00,	10.00,	15.00,	20.00
2,"Cricket Supplies	","00060	""Cricket Bats – Large	""1	32.00,	10.00,	15.00,	20.00
6,"Tennis Supplies	","00070	""Tennis Racket	""1	26.00,	10.00,	15.00,	20.00
6,"Tennis Supplies	","00080	""Tennis Balls	""1	1.20,	5.00,	7.50,	10.00
3,"Soccer Supplies	","00090	","Soccer Ball	""1	18.00,	5.00,	10.00,	15.00
6,"Tennis Supplies	","10010	","Tennis Play Kit	""1	50.00,	5.00,	7.50,	10.00

Fig 9.4

Word processors and desktop publishing applications can also benefit from Sage output. In this instance all you need to do is output the data to a file. The output file can then be read by most word processing and desktop publishing packages. You will only need to remove some odd characters in the file that are placed there by Sage to control the printed output.

Text Editor If you do not have a word processing application, then you can use a text editor that comes with the Sage package. This allows you to create new documents or alter and inspect previously-saved documents and reports. From the **Utilities** menu you select **Text Editor**. You must then enter a filename of an existing file if you wish to edit one previously created or a different filename if you want a new one created. Figure 9.5 shows a report file loaded into the text editor and ready for editing.

| Filename : REPORT.005 | Line : 1 | Column : 1 [I] Memory (K): 395 |

```
^[R^C^C
MEGAXAN STERLING SPORTS                           Sales Ledger Reports        ver

                                    Turnover     Turnover
A/C    Account Name                 YTD          MTH
------ ---------------------------- ------------ ------------
0020   Jackson General Sports       240.00       395.00
0030   Harriers Football Club       468.09       468.09
0040   Dipple Store                 519.73       519.73
0050   Sports Super Centre          507.45       507.45
0060   Howes Gym Centre             340.00       340.00
0070   Minerva Football Co. Ltd.    478.56        68.56
                                    ------------ ------------
                                    2553.83      2298.83

^L^[@
```

Control codes list: ^@ ^A ^B ^C ^D ^E ^F ^G ^H ^I ^J ^K ^L ^M ^N ^O ^P ^Q

Fig 9.5

When you press function key **F4**, you get a list of control codes from which you can select for inserting into your file. These codes are used to effect the printing of the document. When you use the text editor to alter stationery layouts, you use a different way of accessing the text editor. The F4 key in stationery layout gave you a list of field names, while the text editor here gives the control codes for the printer. Apart from this difference, the text editor's operation and use is exactly the same as for stationery layouts.

DATA FILES

At this stage it is worth becoming more familiar with the types of files generated and used by the Sage system. Before going further, be sure you are aware of some of your basic operating system commands (probably MS-DOS). An understanding of the operating system, although not essential to working with Sage, is very useful.

File types

On inspection of directories, you will observe that all files that are either part of or created by the Sage system have a file extension to them such as .DTA. Files contain two elements to their directory entry:

a   A filename, which will be to the left of the decimal point. In MS-DOS this is limited to a maximum of 8 characters

b   A file extension, which will be to the right of the decimal point. In MS-DOS this is limited to a maximum of 3 characters

Such file extensions are designed to tell us and the computer something about the data stored in the files.

Files with the extension EXE represent the program files that make up the Sage system. For example, the file called SAGE.EXE is the program that is initially loaded into the computer when the package is first run.

The files with the extension DTA are used to store the accounts data generated by the program. The filenames indicate what data is stored in them. These files are stored in directories, such as COMPANY0. Later in this chapter you will see that it is possible to have many different sets of company accounts set up on the computer which can be used by the same Sage programs. It is these files that need to be backed up regularly so there is another copy in the event of lost or damaged files.

Figure 9.6 shows a summary of the kind of files used by Sage and where they are stored. The number of such files will depend on the version of Sage you are using and the size and number of accounts or businesses you are working with. Figure 9.6 also suggests how often you should backup such files. Much of the backing up can be done through the Sage Utilities menu rather than through the operating system, which requires a good knowledge, for example, of MS-DOS.

Altering control accounts

Sage allows you the option of changing the way your control accounts are stored. This is not possible using the Nominal Ledger, but it is possible using **Data File Utilities** from the Utilities menu. By selecting **Control Accounts** you can make alterations to any of the control accounts.

If you want to add new bank accounts, then this option allows you to define other accounts. Throughout the working of the program, each time you post details to a bank account (when making a payment for example) you can

File Extension	Purpose	Directory	Back up Priority
.exe	main program files	/SAGE	Once
.dta	company data	/SAGE/COMPANY/ACCDATA	Regularly
.let	letter details	/SAGE/COMPANY	When altered
.lyt	document details	/SAGE/COMPANY	When altered
.hlp	Sage help information needed by Sage	/SAGE	Once
.ins	Installation details	/SAGE	Once
.ovl	Overlay (screen) information for Sage	/SAGE	Once
.prn	Printer information needed by Sage	/SAGE	Once
.psw	Password details	/SAGE	Once
.rep	Report Generator details for Sage	/SAGE	When altered

Fig 9.6

select the bank to which you post the details. With only one bank account, no choice is possible. A Mispostings Account is used in the same way as a Suspense Account, to balance the accounts in the short term and at month end or year end to be altered with the help of Journal Entries to leave no balance.

The other control accounts that can be added to or redefined are the **Bad Debt Write Off Account**, **Depreciation Account**, **Prepayment Account** and **Accruals Account**.

Making global changes

This can be extremely useful and save a good deal of time and effort. The activity allows you to make general changes to data stored in files. For example, if you want to raise all stock prices by 10%, then select from the **Data File Utilities** menu the **Global Changes** option. From here you would select **Stock File Changes**, as this is where the prices are stored. Now you select the field you want altered as **Sale Price**. Finally you select **Increase By %** and enter **10**.

This can be used on many different occasions, for example to increase all credit limits by a given percentage in the Sales Ledger or to alter discount rates.

When using such an option, it is always wise to backup your data files *before* starting in case anything should go wrong.

Correcting posting errors

Sage has the facility to allow you to correct or reverse a posting that was incorrectly entered. To use this you should extract an Audit Trail from the Utilities function because, to alter a posting, you will need to know the transaction number. From the **Utilities** menu select **Posting Error Corrections** and then decide whether you want to correct a posting or reverse it.

If you correct a posting, the details of the transaction will be displayed, leaving you with the job of entering the correct figures. The alterations are then made automatically to the accounts, with details of the corrections remaining as part of the Audit Trail. If instead you reverse the posting, then all the accounting procedures are executed automatically in a way that effectively cancels the transaction.

In both cases it does not lose all trace of a transaction as this would be bad bookkeeping practice. When errors are made, the appropriate transactions should be made to correct them and not simply to wipe them out.

USING MULTIPLE ACCOUNTS

Users of Sage's **Financial Controller** have the facility to work on several different sets of company accounts, useful for a group company with a number of subsidiaries. Setting up the multiple accounts requires directories for more than one company.

The first stage is to create the company sub-directories where the company files will be saved. From the main directory the Sage files will be stored in a directory normally called 'SAGE'. In this directory are sub-directories for the companies starting with COMPANY0 and going through COMPANY1 to COMPANY9. You will need to create COMPANY1, COMPANY2 and any others yourself using MS-DOS commands. Sage only creates COMPANY0 when it is first installed. Consequently, Sage allows you to work with up to 10 different companies.

The next stage is to create the relevant company files. There is a program called MULTICO which has to be run from the operating system. Exit Sage through the menus. You are now in the operating system. (To run MULTICO, you will need to consult your installation guide or whoever installed the program for you.) When running this program you will be asked for details about each company which should be entered. Not until such company details have been entered should you quit the program.

Once you have completed the details and quit from the main menu, you are in a position to run Sage and select which company you want to work on.

When you next use Sage it will seek out a file called COMPANY. If the file does not exist, then it assumes you are working with a single company system and carries on with asking for the password. If the file does exist and you have entered the details correctly, then a list of companies will appear offering you the choice of which company to work with.

This facility can be of particular use in a training environment where you want to work on different companies on a network system. It is also of use when a business has organised the accounts system into distinct departments or cost centres. If the accounts of the different companies have to be **consolidated**, it is important that, when you set up the extra companies, one of them is defined as a parent company and the others as subsidiaries.

A useful way of using the different companies option is to set up each month as a different 'company'. At the end of each month, prior to clearing the files down, you can copy the current month into another 'company'. With up to 10 different companies allowed, you can keep a fairly extensive history of accounts, giving you the opportunity to skip back a few months when required and avoid the cumbersome task of restoring past backups.

SAGE PERISCOPE

The situation often arises where you are working in a different package, such as in word processing, and want to look at the Sage accounts without having to leave the package. Sage offers just that kind of facility with its Periscope program.

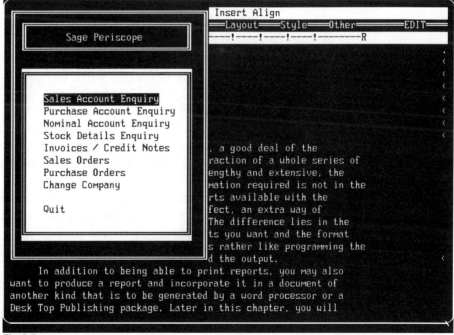

Fig 9.7

Within the Sage directory is a program called **View**. To activate this, type VIEW from the DOS prompt and the program is loaded into memory for future use. When working in another program, you simply press the **Alt** and **Enter** (Return) keys together. Figure 9.7 is an example of the opening menu of Periscope when activated from within a word processing package.

The options are fairly easy to follow but only allow the facility of enquiring on accounts rather than actually processing anything. The information available should be quite adequate for most users' needs. The option also allows you to select a company.

BACKING UP AND RESTORING FILES

As mentioned before, the need to backup files cannot be overstated, for a number of reasons of which the main ones are:

- In the event of lost or corrupt data files, the backup files can always be used with loss only of the information input since the last backup copy was taken.

- In the future you may want to restore files in order to check on a past event.

- You may want to transport data from one machine to another. If, for example, your accountant uses Sage and is happy to work on your accounts data for final auditing, then you could send a copy of a backed set of your data files. Alternatively, you might have another computer at home with Sage on and you are then able to take copies of the entire companies' data to your other machine. Remember, it is always safer to move data around rather than the machines!

Backing up

This option appears on the Utilities menu and works in exactly the same way as backing up at the end of each session. If you backup on to either a floppy disk or the same hard disk, the files with 'dta' extensions are copied to make files with a 'bak' extension.

You should always backup regularly, with most businesses needing to backup files at least once a day while the computer is in use. At the end of each period, normally monthly, you should backup on to another disk and label it with the month and year. Keep this disk in case you need to restore it.

Restoring from a back-up

Restoring from backed up files is virtually the opposite of the backing up procedure and is done in almost the same way. Before restoring you should note that the system will copy all 'bak' files from a previously backed up set of files to 'dta' files, wiping out the existing 'dta' files in the process. If the existing ones are corrupt, then this may be intended. If you are restoring from a previous month only because you want to make an enquiry, ensure that you backup the current month *before* restoring.

When you select this option from the **Utilities** menu, you will see details of the last 10 backups. You can restore from any backup and this list is for information purposes only. If you backed up on to a floppy disk, then you will be prompted for the disk to be placed into the drive.

As a word of caution, do not attempt to use the operating system to restore selective files. Much of the data in different files will be related in some manner and to restore one set of files and not another could lead to the program having severe difficulties in operating correctly. In general, it is wise to backup and restore everything each time.

IMPORTING DATA

A useful, and in some situations vital, facility of Sage is to import data from another source. File import allows you to convert data stored in comma separated value format in files. In Figure 9.4 earlier in this chapter you saw an example of Sage output to such files. Now the process is reversed to import data because Sage collects such data and inserts it all correctly into its own files.

A business using Sage for the first time may have a good deal of information in computer form already. It may then be possible for this information source to be output in such a way that Sage will be able to import it. Also, many suppliers of stock are able to send stock details on disk in a format which enables you to import it into your Sage files. Before you do this, you might have to make some amendments to such a file. One way of doing this might be to load such data into a database package, such as dBase or DataEase, alter the record structure so that Sage can accept it and then output the data to a comma separated value file ready for import.

You will observe that the comma separated value file is organised so that each complete line is a record. On each line a COMMA is used to separate the records into fields. Each line must have the same number of fields. If the field is to store non-numeric data (alphanumeric), then the data must be between parentheses (data). Another condition for importing data into Sage is that the sequence of fields in each record must match that expected by Sage.

Sage allows you to import data into *six* different sets of files: Sales Accounts, Purchase Accounts, Nominal Accounts, Transactions Records, Stock Records and Stock Transactions. Figure 9.8 sets out the structure required for a comma separated file so Sage can import data into either the Sales or Purchase Ledger Accounts. Such a list could come from a list previously stored in a word processor or database package. The important point to understand is that you might have to do some work on the file before it is ready to import.

Files	Field sequence for the Comma Separated Value file	Numeric or alphanumeric
Sales Account	Account reference	Alphanumeric
	Account name	Alphanumeric
	Address line 1	Alphanumeric
	Address line 2	Alphanumeric
	Address line 3	Alphanumeric
	Address line 4	Alphanumeric
	Telephone number	Alphanumeric
	Contact name	Alphanumeric
	Analysis code	Alphanumeric
	Discount code	Alphanumeric
	Credit limit	Numeric
	Turnover	Numeric
Purchase Account	The format needed for this file is similar to that needed for the Sales Account	

Fig 9.8

If data for any of the fields is not available, then you will have to insert a space or a zero, depending on the value type, and not simply leave the field out. For the import to work, you must have the required number of fields and in the correct sequence.

Importing data into the Nominal Accounts works in exactly the same way. The sequence is set out in Fig 9.9. As you will observe, very little appears because importing such data simply sets up the nominal structure. Any transactions data must be imported with a different structure.

Field sequence for the Stock file	Numeric or alphanumeric
Account reference	Alphanumeric
Account name	Alphanumeric
Month 1 budget	Numeric

Months 2 to 12 budget fields are needed, making a total of 14 fields to complete the required Comma Separated Value file

Fig 9.9

The Transactions file will normally require a little more work to make the data compatible for import, because Sage recognises only specific transaction type codes. Figure 9.10 lists the codes, while Fig 9.11 sets out the required structure.

Transaction type codes	Transaction
SI	Sales invoioo
SC	Sales credit
PI	Purchase invoice
PC	Purchase credit
BP	Bank payment
BR	Bank receipt
CP	Cash payment
CR	Cash receipt
SA	Sales payment on account
PA	Payment on account

Fig 9.10

File sequence for the transactions	Field type
Transaction type	2 letter code
Sales or Purchase Account reference	Alphanumeric
Nominal Account reference	Alphanumeric
Departmental code	Numeric 0–9
Date	Alphanumeric
Transaction reference	Alphanumeric
Details of transaction	Alphanumeric
Nett amount	Numeric
Tax code	2 digits (T0, T1)
Tax amount	Numeric

Fig 9.11

The remaining two files are related to stock. The Stock Record file refers to standing data that is entered when a stock record is initially set up. The transaction file holds details about stock movements. The types of transaction are:

AI   Adjustments In
AO   Adjustments Out
GI   Goods In
GR   Goods Returned

If you have a large supplier that supplies many of your product lines, it is well worth investigating whether they will issue you with a disk containing the stock records. The stock transactions may need more work but if you have sales staff working away from the office selling stock, then they could keep details of this in the form required to import into Sage as stock transactions.

When running this part of Sage, the program will perform two stages. Stage one will examine the file being imported to make certain that it is correct. If there are any errors or inconsistencies, then you will be issued with a report to help you put them right. Stage two will only go ahead if the file is ready for import. This goes through each record line, building up the Sage accounts.

Stock file type	Field details	Field type
Stock records	Stock code	Alphanumeric
	Stock description	Alphanumeric
	Stock category	Alphanumeric
	Departmental code	Numeric 0–9
	Nominal Account reference	Alphanumeric
	Purchase Account reference	Alphanumeric
	Unit of sales	Numeric
	Sales price	Numeric
	Tax code	2 digits (T?)
	Discount rate A	Numeric
	Discount rate B	Numeric
	Discount rate C	Numeric
	Re-order level	Numeric
	Re-order quantity	Numeric
	Supplier part reference	Alphanumeric
	Location	Alphanumeric
Stock transactions	Transaction type	2 digit code
	Stock code	Alphanumeric
	Date	Alphanumeric
	Reference	Alphanumeric
	Details	Alphanumeric
	Quantity	Numeric
	Cost price	Numeric
	Sale price	Numeric

Fig 9.12

On a final point, when data is imported into files, the records are added to the existing ones if the references are different, so that the existing records are not wiped out. This means that you could, for example, add extra stock from suppliers to the stock file. It also means you can update records quickly with new details.

10 Case studies

INTRODUCTION

This final chapter focuses on methods of implementing a computerised system. One of the problems of implementing computerised accounts is that the best strategy for one business may not necessarily be the best for another. Although there are some basic and important rules to observe, it is difficult to state a general set of principles for implementing such a system that can be applied to all businesses. Another problem is that the technology and related software is changing at such a rapid pace that an ideal solution now may not be the ideal solution in a few years' time.

This chapter will present you with three fictitious case histories outlining the way in which three businesses computerised their accounting procedures (and other functions) and the varying degrees of success. At the end of each case study is a series of questions, which are designed to generate thought and/or discussion.

CASE STUDY 1: BRIGHTER LIGHT LTD

This case study is based on a company that manufactures and markets domestic lighting equipment. The equipment manufactured is quite extensive, but the mainstream of activity involves the manufacture of 30 different ranges of torches, 10 different ranges of light fitting, 10 types of table lamps and a range of specialist lights, often made to customer's order.

The company prides itself on meeting orders from retailers and overseas customers promptly and always delivering on time. Some simple facts about the company are given here.

The facts

Number of employees:

Production shop floor	15
Production administration	2
Marketing, sales and distribution	5
Despatch	4

Accounts	3
Managerial	4
Total staff	27

Turnover	£12 million
Expected number of orders	400 per month
Number of suppliers	100
Number of regular customers	650
Average stock value on premises	£2.5 million
Number of different items held in stock	5000

Although these figures depict the state of the company at present, they represent a 50% growth in the volume of trade during the five years since the company was formed.

Projected growth for the next five years is estimated at about 15% to 20% per annum. With such growth, it is anticipated that more capital equipment will be required and there is likely to be a need to employ more production shop floor staff (probably two staff) and an extra person to cope with despatch of goods. The company already has its production staff working on regular overtime and equipment working six days a week when production needs to be high to meet orders, hence the need for more staff and capital equipment.

The problems

All administrative procedures are, at present, done manually by clerical staff. Although the company sees no problem in coping with the extra capital equipment and staff, it anticipates a problem in information flows which cannot be overcome by simply employing more administrative staff. In fact, information needs are not being properly satisfied by the current manual system. The company has identified the following information problems which will get worse with the projected growth:

1   Maintaining efficient stock levels becomes increasingly difficult. With the more essential stock items, such as differing types of flex (there are 50 in all), the company holds far more stock than is probably needed, because it cannot afford to run out. It is estimated that stock values are £500 000 higher than necessary, a figure that may well grow rapidly with expansion.

2   Keeping track of customer orders is becoming a strain, endangering the reputation the company has made for meeting customer orders punctually.

3   At any one time, there are up to 100 purchase orders with a range of suppliers, some of whom are overseas. Keeping checks on suppliers is becoming difficult because the information on orders still outstanding is

coming to the Production Manager too late. On more than one occasion, the manufacture of key products had to be held up because of shortages of certain components. The problem tends to be resolved by resorting to holding even higher stock levels of key components.

4   Information about customers owing money to the company is not forthcoming at the right time. Quite often customer debt is left outstanding longer than it needs to be and customers exceed their credit limits because of lack of information coming fast enough. The average total of customer debt is £1.2 million. It is estimated that this figure could be reduced to an average of £800 000 without damaging company sales. Also, bad debts could fall by half to about £50 000 per annum.

Despite these problems, it is important to stress that the company is far from disaster. However, it sees that, if something is not done about these problems over the next two years, a serious situation could evolve.

The new system

The decision to computerise was taken as a result of a visit by a computer consultant, who advised that the company should acquire the following:

A computer network of four microcomputers. Each microcomputer has its own hard disk with a capacity of 40 megabytes and the file server, where the main files would go, holds up to 70 megabytes of information.

The Sage Financial Controller package.

The strategy was to computerise the stock control function first, as this was identified as the main problem area. A decision could have been made to implement *all* functions simultaneously, but this was felt to be too ambitious. One thing at a time was regarded as the best policy.

When the equipment was installed, one microcomputer was positioned in the Production Manager's office, one in stores and two with the Production administration staff. The file server was also positioned in the Production office where the two Production administration staff were located. The consultant who organised the installation also arranged two days on-site training for the two Production administration staff, the person in charge of stores and the Production Manager. The two-day training was focussed towards setting up and running stock control and purchase order systems.

Getting prepared

The next stage was to place all stock information on to the stock control system. This process took the following form:

1 The person in charge of stores had to ensure that *all* stock cards kept for each item of stock were up to date. There must be one stock card for each item of stock; the description for each item should be correct, cost prices should be accurate and the location where stock could be found should be correct.

   During this exercise, some errors were found and corrected, with improvements being made.

   The company always noted on stock record cards the estimated lead time for ordering stock quantities, re-order quantities, the usual supplier and stock movement history.

2 The production team which was to be responsible for maintaining the stock control system had decided to scan carefully through the stock records, allocating new codes for their own stock items. It was felt that this was long overdue and now was the best time to do this. Essentially, the stock codes that were already in existence would still be used, but each code would be prefixed with A, B, C or Z to indicate the classification of stock. Basically, classification 'A' meant the stock was expensive and should be held only when needed in the short term. At the other end of the spectrum, 'Z' indicated very little cost involved in both buying and holding stock. The purpose of this was to get stock lists in the order they were required, a technique the team learnt during training. Also, the stock code would be a 3-digit code, following the classification code, to indicate where in the warehouse the stock would be located. Again, this produced a listing of stock that would prove useful for stores management, providing 'picking lists' from the Sage Report Generator and a quick check on stock.

3 When everything was complete and, as a result, the data was ready for input, the decision was made to create all the stock records on computer during the weekend. The weekend chosen was soon after the stock manual records were ready; there was always the fear that, if this process were delayed for any time, the figures would soon be out of date. A Saturday was chosen, with four operators working through the day on the four microcomputers, to input the information. Two of the staff needed a little training, but by the end of the day all records were entered on the computer.

At this point, the only item missing on the stock records was the actual stock level. This was intentionally left until last, because a time delay in getting this information on to the computer would render all such stock level figures useless. Before progressing further, a printout of the stock details already entered was extracted and a few alterations were made, as well as adding three records that were originally omitted.

Another visit from their consultant led to the advice that all such records should be backed up before going any further. It was decided that a backup be made to floppy disks immediately, with the disks labelled and dated. In future, backups would be made weekly on to the microcomputer in the Production Manager's office. The Sage backing up procedure was regarded as sufficient for this activity. It was also agreed that such a backing up procedure would be carried out regularly, at the end of each day on to a different machine each time, rotating between the other three machines. The Production Manager has recommended to the Board that, at a future date, the file server should be equipped with a tape streamer that would be capable of backing up everything on the file server at the end of each day within 10 minutes.

Getting started

The next stage was to enter all stock quantities and implement the system. It was decided to do this on the following Friday and Saturday. During these two days, stock levels were checked and stock records adjusted to reflect actual stocks in the warehouse. Each stock record was then given an opening stock using Sage stock control Adjustments In procedure.

The responsibility of keeping stock levels up to date was that of the person in charge of the stock. As from the Monday, every issue or receipt of stock was entered as a stock movement; Adjustment In when stock was received and Adjustment Out when stock was issued. This implementation went extremely smoothly without too much disruption to the normal business. The company went on using the system almost unhindered for a month. It became apparent to the Production Manager that the ability to sit at a terminal and enquire on stock quantities at any time was an invaluable tool for his job, especially when planning production. Also, it was found that the 'low stock' reports were extremely useful when planning what orders to place with suppliers. The consultant had created some special stock reports from the Report Generator to get the kind of reports wanted by the Production Manager.

Only one problem occurred when, in error, the stock files were corrupted on the file server. This happened at 10.45 one morning. The Production Manager telephoned the consultant and soon put things right by restoring the stock details from the previous day (which had been backed up on to his own machine) and re-entering the morning's movement figures. The whole process wasted just two hours, soon recovered during the day's work.

At the end of the month, another stock-take exercise was carried out to see how closely it matched the computer system records. The differences were small and easily corrected and new procedures for the collection and input of data were quickly drawn up.

Further developments

During the month, the Production administration staff were sent on a computer appreciation course for two days. As a result of this, they requested the facility of a word processing package for their machines to replace their typewriters. The Production Manager, commending them for their suggestion and enthusiasm, promptly purchased two single-user versions of WordPerfect for their machines. Within one week, both staff were using their packages in preference to their typewriters. In addition to this, they learnt the technique of outputting reports to a file and then using the word processing package to incorporate the stock control output into reports and letters to a professional standard.

One of the obvious problems with the computerised stock system was the fact that low stocks could not automatically generate an order for new stocks because the system did not take into consideration what was already on order. It was felt, therefore, that the next stage was to implement the Purchase Order system.

The first step was to decide on the preprinted stationery to be used. The existing stationery for generating order forms was scrapped and the company ordered from Sagesoft Ltd their own stationery with their company logo.

When the stationery arrived, adjustments were made to the stationery layout set up in the relevant Sage files. After a few trial and error dummy runs, the printing of orders matched the stationery. One of the Production administration staff placed all outstanding orders on to the system. It was found that printing orders to suppliers using this system was relatively quick and easy, and a substantial improvement on typing orders and placing copies on a file.

Other benefits

Almost immediately, the implementation of the Purchase Order system enhanced the Stock Control system and made it easier to see any outstanding orders that had not been received. Also, the ordering of more stock when stock reached re-order levels was much more efficient. Within a few weeks, staff were becoming more capable and confident with the system, and stocks held on the premises could be reduced, as it was apparent there was less need to hold large stocks.

One of the other benefits derived from the computerisation of both stock recording and purchase ordering was that staff had more time to study the supply of stock and 'shop around' for better quotations from other suppliers.

In all it was estimated that the value of stock in hand fell by £200 000 (saving an estimated £13 000 a year in holding costs) and about £10 000 would be saved in a year because of better terms given by switching suppliers.

System evaluation

The company's Board of Directors, at an evaluation meeting, had come to the conclusion that the computerisation project was a resounding success and should be extended into accounts. The Accounts Manager, therefore, was given the job of investigating the feasibility of computerising the sales, invoicing and sales order processing functions of the business. The reason for this was largely that the Production Manager had complained that the effectiveness of stock control was hindered because it was not clear from the computer what stocks were earmarked for sale. If it were clear what stocks were allocated for sale, it would be easier to decide what needed re-ordering and, more importantly, rational decisions could be made regarding production planning. Too much time was still wasted in switching production schedules at the last minute to meet pressing orders.

Computerising the sales function

The Accounts Manager began by using the same consultant to help decide a strategy on computerising sales. The first stage involved acquiring three extra microcomputers and upgrading the existing file server to enable it to be linked to them. Additional printers were also acquired. One microcomputer was installed in the Accounts Manager's office, one in the main accounts office and one with the sales clerk.

As soon as the system was upgraded and the additional hardware installed, four members of staff, one of whom was the Accounts Manager, were trained on using the computer, and in particular the Sales Ledger functions. A trainer came to the Company and trained the staff on site. The training lasted two days.

Then the four staff formed a small committee, chaired by the Accounts Manager, to decide on a plan of action. The plan decided upon took the following form:

1   Design and order special continuous stationery from Sagesoft for the invoices, credit notes and sales acknowledgement forms.

2   Collect details of *all* customers and input this information to the Sales Ledger, entering an opening balance into each account to indicate how much is owed by each customer.

3   Update the stock files already implemented, so that each stock line has the correct selling price as well as the discount details associated with the line. The VAT codes also need updating as the Production Control Department has not entered the codes for all stock.

4   Enter every invoice, credit note, debit note and all accounts adjustment details to the Sales Ledger.

These first four stages were implemented smoothly, although staff did not appreciate the benefits of entering such details, other than being able to print customer statements of account. This system was left to run for one month before extending it. Meanwhile, the following preparations were being made:

1 Each stock record was being prepared with a departmental code to indicate categories of lights being sold. For example, all table lamps were given department code 1.

2 Each stock item had a VAT code attached to it.

This was all done in conjunction with operating the Sales Ledger by itself for one month. In the second month, the next stage could go ahead.

As each customer was about to be invoiced or sent a credit note, the operator would use the Invoicing function to achieve this. This went ahead with remarkable results. It meant that the stock file was now being updated almost immediately the stock had been issued. In addition to this, the whole process of invoicing had been speeded up. The operators soon got into the habit of processing such transactions as a Batch Processing run at 11.00 am each weekday.

The information being supplied to both the accounts and marketing personnel proved invaluable. In fact, for the first time, the Marketing Department could analyse sales performance almost as soon as it happened.

In addition to this, keeping a more effective check on customer credit limits meant fewer customers were being allowed to go over their credit limits without proper authorisation.

Within one month of this, sales order processing was also implemented. This proved easy because most of the preparation had been done. As a starting point, all outstanding orders were placed on file and then all orders received from customers were processed through the computerised Sales Order Processing system. Operators soon realised the benefits and found themselves with more time to concentrate on customer relations and promoting the company's products.

In addition to many of the accounting functions being carried out, those responsible for maintaining stock levels not only knew what was in stock at any time, but also what was on order and what stock had been allocated to sales.

Completing accounts

After six months of computerisation, a number of minor errors had been ironed out and the company was running the system with a good deal of success.

The next stage in the development of the system was to extend the role of computerised accounts to include both the Nominal Ledger and Purchase Ledger.

Starting with the Nominal Ledger, the company soon had this function set up and integrated with the rest of the operation. All Journal entries were, at first, carried out by the Accounts Manager. The first set of automatic postings from the Sales Ledger to the Nominal Ledger caused a few problems, but these were soon sorted out. Most Journal entries were set up through recurring entries, depreciation automation, and Prepayment and Accruals.

Further development

After 18 months the company had seen its information systems develop a long way. One of the main future developments would be to extend the size of the system to allow more users to access the information on the system. The marketing personnel's information requirements are such that they need a good deal of information on sales. A microcomputer has been installed in their office to facilitate this requirement.

Over time, as the system developed, the company organised itself quite effectively in order to get data on to the computer as quickly and simply as possible.

The major problem caused by computerisation is that the company now finds it much more difficult to recruit staff of the right calibre, even when it has increased its staff salaries to reflect the additional skills required to perform the tasks.

At present the company has computer expertise among its managers, who have a number of developments they wish to get under way, Payroll almost certainly being the next project. It is anticipated that the information processing requirements over the next few years will go on changing.

The latest evaluation report shows that the company is meeting its information needs well and would be able to cope easily with future expansion.

Case study questions

1   Trace the history of Brighter Light's computerisation, indicating timescales involved. When doing this, try to show the development as a diagram depicting the sequence of events with timescales.

2   What role did staff training take in the development exercise and to what extent did it help?

3   Could the company have started with computerising the accounts function first, followed by stock control, in much the same way as covered in this book?

4   What developments can you see in the future for this company?

5   Outline:

  a   The benefits of the new system
  b   The costs of the new system

CASE STUDY 2: DALEK STATIONERY SUPPLIES

This case study is based around a firm that supplies stationery through one retail outlet and also distributes supplies direct to a large number of businesses and individuals. The firm has three categories of clientele:

1 Customers through its retail outlet
2 Corporate organisations who are supplied in bulk and receive sizable discounts
3 Small firms and individuals who order goods based on a widely distributed catalogue – mail order

Although this firm has a large customer base, its supplier base is relatively small. There are three large UK-based businesses and about 15 overseas businesses who supply to the firm via agents; this avoids the firm having to handle import procedures.

The facts

The following facts will help give some perspective on the firm.

Number of employees:

Retail staff	2
Driving and despatch staff	2
Storekeeper	1
Administrative staff	2
Managerial staff	1
Total staff	**8**

Turnover	£2.4 million
Expected number of orders	250 per month
Number of suppliers	18
Number of regular customers – corporate	26
mail order	800
Average stock value on premises	£150 000
Number of different items held in stock	2000

Background

The business has developed over four years of trading and was founded by its Manager, Jack Staples. The business has grown rapidly, with the mail order side of the business being the latest activity, launched one year ago.

Staples envisages that the retailing and corporate sides of the business will grow less than 5% per annum over the next three years. On the other hand, if it can get its marketing and distribution right, the mail order side could double over the next two years.

In order to develop the mail order side of the business, Staples believes that the sales side of the business will need to be computerised in order to cope with the growth in administrative activity.

Getting started

Staples takes the following action:

1   He organises national newspaper and magazine advertisements for his catalogues. The advertisements are designed to appear at the same time in all the publications in one month's time.

2   He orders from his printers a new set of catalogues.

3   He buys a microcomputer with a 20 Mbyte hard disk, colour screen and a printer. The microcomputer is one of the latest and looks extremely stylish; he is always fussy about appearance.

4   He purchased a copy of Sage Accountant through a Sage dealer. He learnt about this package from an accountant friend at his Golf Club who used Sage for other business accounts.

After receiving delivery of the computer hardware and software, Staples spent many hours struggling with the manuals to get the system set up and installed. Eventually, with a little help from a friend and a few telephone calls to the dealer who sold him the computer system and software, he got Sage correctly installed.

After two weeks of having the system, he decided to appoint one of his administration staff, Judy Punch, to operate the Sage system. Judy was sent on a three-day course to learn about the Sage package. Because the course did not start exactly when he needed, four weeks had passed before Judy went on the course. This coincided with the advertisements for the mail order side of the business. On top of the normal business load, Judy was away on the three-day Sage course, and requests for 3000 catalogues had suddenly accumulated. All staff were now working overtime in order to get the catalogues delivered, with some orders from existing customers being held up for a day or two.

When Judy returned from her course she was required to set up the Sage system with a view to implementing the Sales Ledger immediately, to incorporate the new customer accounts on the mail order side of the business. Judy spent many hours setting up the Sales Ledger and entering all the customer details for existing mail order customers. The time spent doing this meant further neglect of other processing activities in the firm; again orders were being delayed, because invoices were not being set up correctly.

Crisis management

After another two weeks, new customer orders were coming in at about 90 a day, and the administration could not cope. Staples, in a near state of panic, contacted the local job agency and recruited two temporary staff to help handle the requests for catalogues, production of invoices and some basic accounts work for the shop. In addition to this, he employed the services of a consultant from a neighbouring firm who was experienced in setting up computerised accounts for such firms.

With the help of two temporary staff, who needed a good deal of supervision, and the consultant, a plan of action was drawn up.

The two staff in the shop concentrated on managing the shop and doing something about getting the backlog of work sorted out. Many stocks were low in the shop by now and disgruntled customers were complaining of some stocks not being available. In addition to this, some accounts work had been neglected.

The two temporary staff and the other administrator concentrated on getting the mail order and corporate customer orders backlog sorted. This largely involved getting orders processed and invoices made up so that goods could be despatched. The storekeeper and drivers concentrated on coping with the extra despatches. A much larger proportion of despatches had to be sent by post in order to cope with the extra work.

During all this activity, Judy Punch was able to get the Sales Ledger set up properly and enter all invoices through the Sales Ledger. By the end of the second month, the processing was up to date and customers received their first computerised set of statements of account.

Getting settled

It was difficult to assess whether any real damage had been caused by the introduction of a computer and the transition period that occurred. However, Staples felt certain that some ground had been lost with some of the mail order customers, and orders were lost with two large corporate customers. In addition to this, Staples spent a good deal of money employing staff for overtime work, employing temporary staff and paying consultancy fees. It is also certain that his advertising campaign to expand the mail order side of the business did not have the impact it was designed to have.

However, in spite of everything, growth in business activity was expected, albeit not as large as originally planned. With the help of the consultant he hired, the decision was made to start the Nominal Ledger as soon as staff training was adequate. One of the shop staff was trained on the Sage system, along with Staples himself.

Meanwhile, one of the temporary staff left the firm and the other was taken on full-time; Staples felt the growth in the mail order side of the business now justified the extra member of staff.

Once the training was over, the decision was made to set up and run the Nominal Ledger. On this occasion, the transition went smoothly. It only took a few days to set up the accounts and enter the opening balances. Staples learnt from previous experience and from the training course that adequate pre-planning and preparation was an important factor when converting manual files to computerised ones.

It soon became evident that the system, with only one microcomputer, was not sufficient for the business information requirements. He was advised to install a network of three microcomputers. Consequently, he needed two extra microcomputers and a file server. The new system was set up with two computers placed in the main office and one with the storekeeper for future development. Staples regretted not being able to anticipate this early on, because the adaptation to a network cost more than if he had started with a networked system, and it meant having to retrain staff for the different skills required of them. It also caused a little staff resentment. In addition to the extra hardware, he had to purchase Sage Financial Controller to upgrade his software for the new environment and demands that would be placed upon it.

Very soon after this, both shop workers got used to the computerised system and found that it was saving them time. Also, Staples had learnt how to extract the information he wanted from the Ledgers and was soon planning effectively for changes in sales and keeping closer checks on customer debt.

Expanding the system

After two months, the system had settled well and Staples was ready to utilise the Purchase Ledger, Sales Order Processing, Invoicing and Purchase Order facilities. He sent his storekeeper on a Sage course with the aim of learning how to set up and maintain the stock files needed for the operation of the additional functions.

As soon as the storekeeper felt ready, he began to prepare the stock records by ensuring that all stock cards were complete and accurate. It was decided that stores would be kept separate from the shop stock. When goods were moved from stores to shop, it would be treated as a stock issue from stores in much the same way as issuing stock to customers through mail order. The storekeeper converted all records to the computer in about one month and soon learnt to keep the records updated, especially with prices.

A major problem then occurred because Judy Punch left the firm for another job; she felt that with so much computing expertise behind her she could command a much higher salary than Staples was willing to offer. Staples had to recruit another employee to bring him to full staff strength. Finding another member of staff with the necessary expertise proved difficult. Eventually he found someone, after increasing the salary offered by 20%. This new person still needed training in Sage and needed some time to be able to get to grips with the way the firm went about its business.

The transition period between Judy leaving and the new person being taken on and becoming able to work fully with Sage went on for about two months. During this period, some potential trade was lost, along with credibility with a number of customers. Unfortunately the usual backlog of work had built up. Staff morale had also taken a little knock.

It took nearly three months for the expanded system to finally settle and for all the data processing to be up to date. Much of the management information was only just becoming of real use to Staples.

After one year of computerisation, the firm had expanded its business in all fields, especially the mail order aspect. Staples, on reflection, felt that computerisation was a success but realised that it could have gone much better with more careful planning, better handling of the staffing situation and better use of informed advice.

Case study questions

1 Trace the history of the development of computerisation at Dalek Stationery Supplies, indicating timescales involved. When doing this, try to show the development as a diagram with the sequence of events and the timescales.

2 In your opinion, did Staples start off correctly? Explain the reasoning behind your answer.

3 To what extent did the lack of staff training and involvement influence some of the problems that occurred?

4 At what stage did Staples really get involved with the package? Did it help matters?

5 What can be done to improve staff morale, performance and the likelihood that staff will stay with the firm longer?

6 What developments can you see for the future at this firm?

7 Outline:

a The benefits of the new system
b The costs of the new system

CASE STUDY 3: NATIONWIDE APPLIANCE SUPPLIES plc

This case study is based on a large company that retails durable goods through a national chain of stores. The company has a central headquarters in the north of England, and five regional centres with depots for distributing to retail outlets in each of its regions. The following organisation chart indicates how the company is set up.

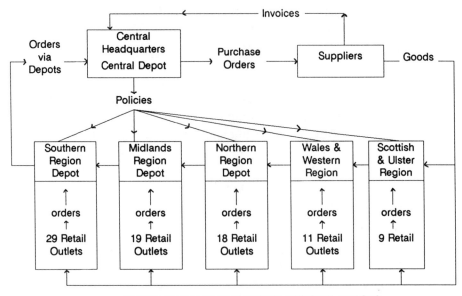

GOODS ARRIVE AT OUTLETS VIA REGIONAL DEPOTS

Fig 10.1

The role of Central Office is to:

1 Make *all* purchasing decisions and order supplies centrally, to ensure maximum discounts from suppliers.
2 Define sales policy, which determines exactly what each retail outlet is to sell and at what price. This ensures the company develops a clear national corporate image and can market its retail outlets in a more effective way.

Each retail outlet is headed by a local manager, with a deputy manager and up to four full-time assistants and part-time staff. The number of staff at each outlet will vary from store to store, depending on the time of year and the size of store.

Local retail managers decide on shop layout, although general guidelines are issued from headquarters. They also order stocks from their regional depot; hire and fire part-time and full-time assistants; and attend weekly regional meetings. Retail managers and their deputies receive basic salaries plus bonuses linked to their retail outlet's sales performance. Also, retail management can find their bonuses suffering if they recruit too many staff to justify the sales volume.

Each region has an area manager and assistant manager, who have the task of co-ordinating the activities within their region; organising and overseeing staff training and development; and managing the distribution of stock. Also, regional centres manage the depots and are responsible for keeping stocks replenished. It is important to note that *all* ordering of stock is done through Central Office. Deliveries, however, from suppliers are made direct to the depots. Area managers meet at headquarters once a fortnight.

The current computer system

Central Office has developed a mainframe computer system based at the headquarters, with minicomputers at each regional depot for the purpose of:

a Overall company accounts
b Stock control
c Purchase Ledger
d Monitoring of sales across the regions and within the retail outlets
e Purchase Order system
f Payroll – this system has been especially developed to ensure that retail managerial staff receive bonuses to match their sales performance
g Monitoring receipts of goods from suppliers to regional depots
h Management information systems

The system has taken ten years to develop to its current stage and will go on being developed by the company for the foreseeable future. Each regional centre's minicomputer has a direct link with the mainframe at Central Office via modem links. The modems enable data transmission between headquarters and each region in much the same way as any other data communication link. The mainframe has a set of modems, one for each region, so that all regional centres can interact with Central Office simultaneously. The company, therefore, has set up for itself a Wide Area Network (WAN).

The software on the system has been tailored by the company's own programming staff. The company employs a Senior Systems Analyst and two junior analysts, whose function is to oversee the entire computer system, its operations and development. There are six computer programmers who work under the supervision and instruction of the Senior Systems Analyst. In addition to this, the company has four maintenance staff who are responsible for ensuring that the computer systems function.

At retail level, there is virtually nothing in the way of computer systems other than electronic tills that keep a simple set of accounts. The Retail Deputy Managers have the responsibility of submitting sales reports each day on specially designed sheets, which are posted to their regional depot.

The problems to overcome

A major problem with the system is that information about stock levels and retail sales can take up to one week to be entered to the computer system. This is because the retail shops have to fill in sales sheets by hand, and then post the sheets to the regional office where the information on the sheets is keyed into the computer. Exactly the same problem occurs when retail managers order stock, as order forms are again completed by hand and sent to the regional depots. In addition to information taking too long to be incorporated in the management information system, it was felt to be too time-consuming for staff at both the regional and retail level.

A feasibility study was commissioned to investigate the possibility of installing computing facilities at retail level with the following terms of reference:

1   To reduce the time lag between sales at retail level and the information being available on the Central Office mainframe computer. ·

2   To allow retail management to place orders with their regional offices by computer link rather than filling in stock requisition sheets.

3   Still to maintain each retail outlet as an entity. That is, to ensure that a complete stock, sales and personnel profile can be kept on each retail outlet. One of the major functions of the management information system at Central Office is to monitor and compare retail performance, analysing national, regional and local trends and other statistical data that require individual retail performance figures.

4   To ensure that any new system can be piloted first, and then phased in over time.

5   To provide information for Retail Managers to assist them in both managing stock and being more effective as a sales centre.

With this brief, a feasibility study team was set up which was chaired by the company's Senior Systems Analyst and made up of the junior analysts, two programmers, three Regional Area Managers and six Retail Managers.

The feasibility study was carried out, with regular meetings being held each month, and each member of the team being given a different task to perform. At the end of six months the team agreed and recommended a strategy to the Board of Directors, which was accepted, for immediate implementation.

The strategy

1   A sample of five retail outlets would be selected to run a pilot scheme where each shop would be equipped with a microcomputer, a modem, printer and communications software.

2   Each microcomputer would have a copy of Sage Accountant Plus,

implementing the functions of Purchase Ledger, Nominal Ledger, Invoicing and Sales Order Processing and Stock Control.

3   Both Managers and Deputy Managers of all retail outlets would go on a week's intensive course in computing with Sage, to be based at one of the regional depots.

4   Managers would then go back to their retail outlets to implement the systems within a specified time.

5   While training was being carried out, two of the programmers would set up the Sage system, with all the required Nominal Codes and Report Generation details, in such a way that the reports would reflect what had to be sent to the regional offices. It was vital that all users of Sage should send compatible reports to Central Office. Such reports would be printed to a spool file and then transmitted from the retail outlet's microcomputer to the regional office down a telephone line via a modem.

6   Managers would be required to meet each month for six months to report on the successes and failures of the new system, drawing on their experiences and contributing ideas about how implementation should take effect in future.

7   After this six-month pilot scheme, the pilot team would submit a report on their experiences, along with recommendations about how the scheme should be implemented universally.

The pilot scheme

The first step was taken by purchasing five microcomputers equipped with hard disks, five printers and five data communication kits. Each machine was fitted with the communication boards that would allow the machine to connect to the telephone system. These communication boards were effectively a modem built into the computer rather than having a separate box. The systems staff then installed an operating system on to each hard disk and tested the computers fully. The Sage software was then installed set up in a way that ensured it was correctly configured for the retail outlets. The analysts also set up with the Report Generator a wide range of reports that would be needed by the regional centres.

The programmers, meanwhile, had to write a suite of programs to enable reports being sent down from each retail outlet to be used to update the main computer files as well as being used to transmit details to Central Office.

Five microcomputer systems were quickly set up and distributed to the five retail outlets that made up the pilot scheme. There was a delay, however, because the software that was being developed for the main computer system took longer than expected to write and test. Once the system was fully tested, the five managers and their deputies could then go on a training course.

The one-week training course went off without too much trouble, although three of the managers complained that too much was being taught in too little time and that they feared they could not remember everything expected of them.

Each manager then went back to their store with clear instructions and deadlines to implement their systems. The instructions, in brief, went as follows:

1 Build up the stock files to reflect current stock situations. Time allowed was one week, after which regular updating would have to be made.

2 In week three implement the Purchase Order system by first placing current outstanding orders on to file and then processing new orders from a low stock list.

3 From week four *all* new purchase orders would be printed to a spool file and then, with the aid of company-written software, transmitted to the minicomputer at regional office.

4 Once the system had settled, each retail outlet should then implement the Nominal Ledger and send a detailed Trial Balance each day to the regional office in the same way orders were sent.

5 In week five the Sales Ledger would be implemented, which meant placing all credit sales and cash sales on to the computer. Existing debtors did not need placing on the system, only new ones. Once done, these details too would be sent to the regional office.

6 Because credit control was handled at regional level, retail outlets would receive details on a daily basis about those customers who had made payments towards their accounts. This meant having to collect data from the regional office, print it and then use the information to update the Sales Ledger.

7 Sales Reports would also be sent to the regional centre on a daily basis as soon as they were available.

In order to ensure that feedback from managers was effective, it was decided that the retail management would meet after the first two weeks to report on their progress.

Feedback

After two weeks the managers met with the systems staff to discuss and share experiences. Out of the five managers, four reported it took longer than one week to get the stock files to a position where they could start regular updating. One of the problems found was that managers were not doing a thorough manual stocktake before building up the files. It was established that the best way to do this was to generate special stock cards with all required fields on the cards and fill these in during stocktaking, recording the date on which the information was compiled. With the larger shops it was felt that conversion should be done in four stages by splitting up the stock into four categories and setting up these categories one at a time. Also, stricter checks were needed on sales, and the figures should be entered into the computer in a more systematic way. In other words, it was necessary to establish a simple routine for updating stock. All retail shops, however, had converted the stock files. The managers decided to meet again in four weeks' time.

At the next meeting all managers reported success in setting up and implementing the Purchase Orders system. One of the retail outlets attempted to print orders to a spool file and send them down a line to the regional office. The attempt failed because the system at the regional centre had not been set up properly to receive the information. When eventually the orders were sent, the software at the regional centre had not been correctly written to translate the information into orders; that is, there were some bugs in the software. At the meeting, the Senior Systems Analyst reported that the problems had been sorted and managers could implement the sending of orders by modem to their regional offices rather than sending them by post or courier.

During the next two months, managers had succeeded in meeting the remaining implementation targets, which were achieved within the predicted time span. The only problem managers really found was that of handling the data communications hardware and software. However, after two months they all felt they had just about mastered the skills needed to operate the system.

The scheme ran for another three months before the next meeting. At this meeting plans were drawn up to implement the new system in every retail outlet in all regions. The members of the meeting agreed to form a Steering Committee to draw up a plan for phasing the new system into the retail outlets. From their own experiences they were able to identify some of the pitfalls to look out for and were better able to define training needs. In addition, all the hardware and software problems had been solved.

Corporate strategy

The plan involved starting off with three outlets per month in the Southern Region; two per month in the Midlands, North, Welsh and Western Regions; and one per month in the Scottish and Ulster Regions.

Implementation would take much the same form as for the pilot schemes, with managers and their assistants first going on a one-week intensive training course before actually implementing the system in their shops. Each manager would also have a well-documented 'action plan' which formed a corporate strategy to work from during the process of transition.

The implementation went ahead, in most cases, extremely well. A good deal of trouble-shooting was needed, especially in handling equipment. Another problem occurred because a few shops experienced a change in management during the transition period; although the situation fortunately never occurred where both manager and deputy left together. During the project, regional meetings were held between retail managers, and the visiting of each other's shops became far more common because managers felt they needed to share and draw upon the experience of others. This extra liaison between managers had a beneficial side-effect, because managers often learnt from each other about new sales skills, marketing techniques and shop layouts.

Case study questions

1   Trace the history of the company's development of computerisation, indicating timescales involved. When doing this, try to show the development as a diagram with the sequence of events and the timescales.

2   How long would the complete computerisation in all retail outlets take?

3   Could the company have either saved time or money developing its own software rather than purchasing a package like Sage to do the job instead?

4   Discuss the role of staff training during the project and how staff training might play a role in the future development of the company.

5   How does this company benefit from having such a large number of retail outlets being computerised compared with a small business that only has one outlet?

6   From your knowledge of Sage, identify those parts of the package that were not used and examine whether there might be a role in the company for some of the other functions available in Sage.

7   What developments can you see for the future in this company?

8   Outline:

   a   The benefits of the new system
   b   The costs of the new system

Glossary of terms

Abort Stopping the execution of a program while it is still running. For example, if you are in the middle of updating a record, you may need to abort to avoid a serious error. In Sage this is usually done by hitting the **Esc** key followed by selecting **Abandon**.

Access To refer to data stored on a file. For example, disk access is needed if a Sales Ledger activity is going to keep customer records updated.

Algorithm A series of instructions set up in logical order designed to perform an activity such as sorting stock records into stock number order. The algorithm will be capable of conversion into a computer program.

Amend The activity of changing a record in a file. For example, altering customer address details in the Sales Ledger is a form of file amendment.

Analyst A person who has the job of separating the parts of various activities, for example a systems analyst, database analyst or cost analyst. System analysts may be concerned with analysing computer-based information systems, or manual systems with a view to computerising them.

Append Add a record to a file, such as adding a new customer record to the Sales Ledger.

Application A specific use to which a computer is put, e.g. payroll, sales, job costing. Such applications are often performed on a computer by a software package, or part of an integrated software package.

Audit Trail Recording a sequence of transactions in such a way that any transaction can be traced back. Audit trails, in this sense, can take the form of printed transactions lists or transactions files. Such audit trails are required to allow auditors to check accounts, or personnel to track errors or restore lost transactions data. Within Sage, it gives a list of transactions in the order in which they were entered into the computer.

Background printing The computer outputs a document to the printer while still allowing an operator to use the computer or terminal to process data on another file.

Backing storage Often referred to as secondary storage, it allows data to be stored on media such as disks for long-term storage purposes, i.e. off-line data storage.

Backup A process of copying all data from one source to another for safe-keeping. This option is offered by Sage when you exit the package.

Bar code Often found on retail products, it consists of a set of preprinted vertical bars that hold information about the product, such as stock number. Bar codes are able to be read quickly by computer, using a bar code reader. Computers can determine a price for the product by accessing a related record in a database.

Batch processing Grouping transactions together and then processing them all in one go. For example, a business may choose to enter all invoice details at pre-defined times in the week, rather than entering them when they arrive from suppliers.

Bootstrap A small program built into the computer that instructs the system about how to set itself up when switched on. Part of the bootstrap program is often held on disk, and must be loaded when the machine is switched on.

Buffer A part of memory used as a temporary store to hold data from an input device. For example, most printers have a buffer memory for storing data prior to printing it. Also keyboards often hold at least one line of data before it is sent to the computer's processor.

Bug An error in a program.

Bus A communication channel which data can travel along. Such communication channels consist of a control bus, data bus, address bus and peripheral bus.

Byte A measure of computer memory, normally containing 8 single bits. Each byte usually represents a single character. See **Kilobyte** and **Megabyte**.

Cache memory A form of buffer memory that works at high speed and is capable of keeping up with the computer's CPU. It acts as a buffer between the CPU and the slower main memory. Because the CPU is not delayed by memory access, processing speed is speeded up. The operating system will load segments of programs into cache memory from disks.

Card reader An input device that reads data from cards. The data on such cards can be in magnetic form or simply holes punched into the cards.

Carriage return A single character sent to the computer represented by pressing the **Return (Enter)** key on the keyboard. This also releases data from the keyboard buffer to the computer's processor.

Central Processing Unit Often referred to simply as the processor, this is the main unit of any computer system. The processor accepts its data from input devices, processes such data and sends it to output devices such as screens and printers, or sends it to backing store for saving.

Character A single element in coded form for the processor, such as a letter or a single number digit. Such characters are normally 8 bits, or one byte, long.

Clock A processor contains an electronic pulse generator that is used to transmit synchronised pulses to different parts of the computer for the interpretation and execution of instructions. Such synchronisation will be set at a speed that determines the computer's *clock speed*. Clock speeds are measured in Megahertz (MHz). The faster the clock speed, the faster the internal processing speed of the computer. For most business applications, it is the access time to disks that is more important to processing speed rather than the clock speed.

Command An instruction to the computer to perform a given task.

Computer aided design (CAD) The use of a computer with graphics software to design by electronic drawing. Main applications areas are in the field of engineering drawing, product design, fashion design and technical drawing.

Computer bureau A commercial enterprise offering computing services to organisations. Many businesses use computer bureaux to manage their payrolls. Some computer bureaux can offer on-line services by installing a terminal at the business's premises and charging for computing time on a time-sharing basis.

Computer output on microfilm (COM) A form of computer output that offers effective long-term data storage which is both compact and durable. Such output is especially useful as a means of archiving data.

Control unit That part of the computer's central processing unit or microprocessor that controls the movements of data within the computer.

Corruption A term used to refer to the loss, or corruption, of data. Data corruption is a particular problem when it occurs on a disk. Such corruption can often render the data useless; hence the importance of regular backing up of data.

Cursor A small image, such as a block or dash on the screen, to indicate where data will be entered from the keyboard.

Daisy wheel printer A type of impact printer that prints characters by striking the character images on carbonated ribbon. The characters appear on the end of spokes on a small wheel. The printed characters are of a high quality, but the print style is limited to the characters on the wheel. Particularly good for letter or report writing.

Data An element that will need processing to form the basis of information. It can take the form of an electronic pulse, a magnetic particle, a hole in a piece of paper, a particle of light or any other physical form that can be represented in one of two states. It is the pattern of these data that will be processed by the computer.

Data capture The way in which data is collected or input for processing. Methods of data capture can vary, including entering data with bar code readers, scanners, optical character recognition, or keying in from source documents. The methods of direct input to the computer are increasing, as data capture is often the most time-consuming and error-prone part of general data processing operations.

Database The collection, in a structured form, of all data that represents the basis of information for an organisation's business applications. Most of the Sage data are stored in various directories and recognised by the '.DTA' file extension.

Database management system (DBMS) Software that manages computerised databases, such as updating, creating and interrogating. Such software also manages data storage, and data security and integrity.

Datel The Post Office data transmission facility available to commerce and industry. It allows the transmission of data on either private or public telephone lines. Datel offers a wide and varied service to meet the needs of differing data communication systems.

Dedicated computer A computer system set up to perform one specific task or set of tasks, e.g. a cash dispenser, electronic cash till.

Default A function which is preset. When offering a choice to users the software program assumes the default value if no choice is made.

Diagnostic routine A program used to detect errors in either existing software or hardware. Many diagnostic routines will operate in a way that does not interfere with normal operations and is not apparent to a user.

Disk drive A peripheral device for storing data generated by the computer's processor and for retrieving data by the processor. Disk drives can contain either floppy disks or hard disks.

Disk operating system (DOS) Part of the software that is contained on disk, loaded into computer memory and used to operate the computer system.

Down time The amount of time when a computer is not functioning.

Download The process of loading a program into computer memory.

Driver A part of the operating system software that is used to control certain peripheral devices.

Dual inline package (DIP) An integrated circuit having two rows of connector pins. Most printers have DIP switches which allow settings to be altered so that the connections to the computer are made compatible with both the hardware and software.

Duplex A communications concept that allows simultaneous data transmission down a line in both directions.

EFTPOS This stands for Electronic Funds Transfer at Point Of Sale. It allows funds to be transferred by computer from a customer's account to a trader's account when a transaction takes place, instead of paying with cash or a cheque.

Electronic mail The process of transmitting messages and correspondence between computers electronically. Such mail can be stored for future reference or to be read on screen at a later date.

EPOS Electronic Point of Sale, such as check-out systems in supermarkets that can scan bar codes and price the products. Many such terminals can now perform database activities.

Exception reporting A process of reporting any circumstances that are unusual or not normally permitted. For example, reporting large customer orders or very low stock levels on items of stock.

Expert system A software orientated system which enables a computer to diagnose problems if given the symptoms. Such expert systems often contain information about past events and calculate likely causes of problems through statistical analysis.

Fibre optics A cabling medium for transmitting data. As an alternative form to coaxial cable, it transmits data via light pulses and allows a much greater capacity and is more reliable than coaxial cable.

Field An element of a record that is a collection of characters such as those which make up a customer name or stock number.

File A collection of records that are related in some way. A stock file, for example, may be a collection of stock records.

File protection A method of protecting files from corruption or accidental erasure. A common way of protecting a file is to write protect it, which means files can be read but not written to.

Firmware Software that is set on Read Only Memory and can be easily replaced in the computer. It offers a reliable source of software and is particularly useful when an application is used often.

Floppy disk A backing store medium used to store data. Such disks require to be placed in a disk drive so that the computer can both read from them and write to them.

Flowchart A diagrammatic form for showing functions and sequences of events within a system or sub-system. Such flowcharts take different forms, e.g. program flowcharts depicting the way a program runs or systems flowcharts showing the way a system works.

Form feed A process where a printer *feeds* a sheet of paper through the printer. This is often used to align continuous paper on a printer to the top of the next sheet.

Format The way data is structured on disk, paper or screen. With respect to disks, it is important that new disks are formatted so that they are compatible with the computer system before they can be used.

Fourth generation language (4GL) A programming language that has a high-level structure allowing programming to be done by statements in ordinary English language. A 4GL has normally been tailored for certain applications, such as database.

Front-end processor A method where some processing on a large computer system is done by terminals or microcomputers, e.g. screen layouts, communications transmission, editing, data validation and verification.

Function A general term used to identify a specific group of related tasks, such as the accounting function, stock control function or payroll function.

General purpose computer A computer that can be adapted to a wide range of applications by loading the appropriate software.

Generation of files Often referred to as the grandfather-father-son principle, creating a generation of backed up files. With the cost of storage being relatively cheap, it is often prudent to keep many past generations of backed up files.

Hacking A term used for the act of trying to gain unauthorised access to computerised information, such as using modem equipment to try to gain access to private information held on computer databases.

Half duplex A process of data transmission where data can be sent in both directions down a communication line, but *not* simultaneously.

Handshaking A process where both computer and peripheral tell each other that data transmission is ready to commence. A printer requires this because it is normally unable to print data as fast as it can receive it, so the principle of handshaking ensures items of data are sent down as and when the printer is ready, thereby preventing loss of data.

Hard copy Printed output from a computer.

Hardware The physical attributes of any computer system.

High level language A programming language that is constructed of statements containing ordinary English words. Such high level languages vary in type and sophistication. Examples are: COBOL, Basic, Pascal, C, Fortran and Modula-2.

Housekeeping A term to describe the practice of removing unwanted information from disks and tapes. Good housekeeping will prevent disks from becoming cluttered, speed up processing and lessen the chance of filling up a disk unnecessarily.

IBM The trading name for International Business Machines.

ICL The trading name for International Computers Limited.

Icon A pictorial representation of programs, document files and options available for executing or processing. Icons are often used as an alternative to text menus and directories.

Image processing A process of transmitting, in digitised form, pictures and images.

Impact printers A category of printer that creates images on paper by physically hitting the paper, such as matrix or daisy wheel printers.

Ink jet printer A type of non-impact printer where the characters are produced on the paper by use of a fine jet of quick-drying ink to give high-quality print.

Interface A general term used to describe the processing of data between two systems or sub-systems. For example, a disk interface refers to the transferring of data from processor to disk and back. Such interfaces are collections of both hardware and software.

Job In a computing context, this refers to either the routines or applications being run on a computer system at any one point in time.

Job costing The process of attributing costs against a specific job. In accounting terms, this could be a specific contract or the manufacture of a particular product.

Key field A field within a record that identifies the record itself and is used to access the record.

Keyboard One of the most used forms of input device.

Kilobyte (K) Used to measure data quantity, this represents 1024 bytes of data.

Kimball tag Either pre-punched or magnetised card containing information about an item. Often seen in retail outlets, and used as a storage medium that can hold details about a product. An appropriate computer input device can then read them.

Laser printer A type of non-impact printer giving high quality printed output. Its technology is based on techniques similar to photocopiers.

Line printer Low quality, very high speed printers that print complete lines at a time.

Local Area Network (LAN) A system that connects a number of microcomputers together so that they can share common resources such as a database or printer. While resources can be shared, each computer on a network is still able to act independently of the others.

Logging in A method of getting access to the information stored on a computer. Designed for security, the process of logging in requires an operator to enter identification and, normally, an associated password.

Logging out Signing off a system; an activity that should be carried out whenever an operator has finished their work on a computer.

Magnetic disks A storage medium for data which fits into a disk drive. There are many different types of disk suitable for different types of application and computer systems.

Magnetic ink character recognition (MICR) Typically used by the banks, magnetic ink characters are read by the computer as a way of inputting data to the computer. Magnetic characters appear on the bottom of cheques and are used to assist banks in processing a large volume of cheques.

Magnetic tape A form of backing storage medium where data is placed on tape drives which can store data serially. Magnetic tapes offer an effective and cheap form of backup storage for systems with a large amount of data. They are also used for storing programs that are subsequently loaded into computer memory.

Mainframe computer An exceptionally large computer often capable of supporting many hundreds of computer terminals, microcomputers, storage units, printers and other peripherals. Quite often mainframe computers are used as a large central processor supporting remote systems by data communication links across long distances.

Management information system (MIS) Often used in conjunction with other data processing activities, this system extracts a whole series of reports. With most MIS packages users are able to identify their own information needs and extract reports to meet these.

Matrix printer An impact printer that creates an image on paper through a dot pattern on a matrix. Such matrix printers are effective for printing graphics as well as near letter quality text, at low cost. They are usually adequate for most smaller businesses using computers for accounts, word processing and management information.

Megabyte 1024 Kilobytes.

Merge Combining two related files, normally with the same structure if they are data files, to create one larger file, e.g. to combine a letter and an address list for a mailing.

Microprocessor The more common description for the processing unit of a microcomputer.

Minicomputer Similar to a mainframe computer but on a smaller scale. The distinction between a mainframe and minicomputer is not an obvious one, but minicomputers are often multi-user/tasking machines that can support many peripherals (about 100) on both a local or distributed processing basis.

Modulator/demodulator (MODEM) A device which is connected to a computer for both sending and receiving signals down a telephone line, allowing data communication between computer devices. Such modems will be needed at both ends of a line to allow data communications to work.

Module A function within a program package that can often be used in isolation from other modules. For example, in the Sage system there is a Payroll and Job Costing module that can be purchased and added to the system.

MS-DOS A trade name for MicroSoft Disk Operating System.

Multiplexer A communications device that receives data from a number of computer devices and then sends such data down *one* telephone line. There will be a slowing down in data communications transmission from each device as more of them transmit data, but such devices can reduce the costs of data communications quite considerably.

Off-line A general term referring to data or part of computer system being inaccessible. Data on a disk which is not in the computer disk drive is said to be off-line.

Off-line data processing A process of working on data away from the main computer system or, say, on a microcomputer before interacting with the main system. With the cost and power of microcomputers, it often makes sense to prepare data, such as invoices, off-line and then batch process the work to a mainframe or minicomputer later. Off-line processing can also involve many manual operations, in preparation and validation of data, before computerised (on-line) processing.

Operating system Software that is used to operate the computer and its peripherals.

Operator A term used to describe a person who operates a computer. This is different to the computer programmer who programs a computer.

Optical character reader (OCR) A computer input device that recognises characters, usually in typed form. These can be a considerable labour-saving device when text that has already been typed needs to be entered to the computer.

Parallel running The process of running two systems at the same time; typically a computer system and a manual system. This may be a necessary prerequisite to automating a manual process. Such parallel processing will help to detect errors or bugs in the new system. Eventually, one of the systems will usually be discontinued.

Password A way of ensuring that only authorised personnel have access to parts of a system. Passwords are only effective if they are kept secret from everyone except authorised persons. Passwords are also set up to ensure that different people have access to different parts of the system.

Payroll The function of paying employees, for which computers can be particularly useful, with direct transfer of funds rather than handling large amounts of cash.

Peripheral device Input, output and storage devices that constitute part of a computer system's hardware.

POS Point-Of-Sale.

Prestel A public database service offered by British Telecom.

Protocol The communications protocol is a standard of data communications that tries to ensure compatibility in the way data is communicated across telephone lines.

Random file A file organisation principle that allows the computer direct access to any record without having to read all records preceding it sequentially. Such files are normally stored on disk.

Read/write heads A device contained within a disk drive or tape drive that either reads data into the computer or writes data on to a storage medium from the computer.

Real-time processing Ensuring files and databases are updated by transactions as they occur. To achieve real-time processing when operating a computer system is just as important as having the hardware and software capabilities to do it.

Remote job entry (RJE) This is the process of entering data to computer where the entry point is geographically separate from the central processing unit. RJE is typified by a remote terminal being linked by modem to mainframe or minicomputer.

Report generator A part of a software package that allows users to design their own reports based on their information needs. It allows much greater freedom in the way a user can extract data from the system.

ROM (Read Only Memory) A part of the memory in a computer used to store programs in a permanent way. Part of a computer's operating system (e.g. BIOS) is stored on this. Some systems will also have applications software built into ROM.

Run The actual execution of a program.

Scheduling A process of determining the order in which jobs are performed or executed. Such activities can be done automatically or by the operator, with priorities being set on certain jobs. This tends to be important when working on network systems.

Scrolling A process of text running up or down the screen when you want to view data below or above that shown on the screen. The alternative to scrolling is to clear a screen in such a way that one complete screen at a time can be viewed.

Sequential access A file reading method where data are read in a defined sequence. With magnetic tape, the order of sequential access is the order in which data was saved. Programs are also read sequentially on whatever medium they are stored. Some files support an index which allows files to be read in different sequences.

Sequential file A file where data is stored physically in the order in which it is generated.

Silicon chip A small piece of silicon-based material used to hold computer circuits in a microprocessor. New technology has allowed many thousands of transistors and diodes to be stored on one single chip.

Simplex transmission A method of data communication where transmission of data can be made in *one direction only*.

Soft copy A term used for screen output.

Software All computer programs from operating system to applications software.

Sort A data processing term used when rearranging files into a different order.

Source code The program as written by a computer programmer before it is compiled to form the object code. High level languages, for example, are first written in source code and the computer uses a compiler to convert this source into something from which it can run.

Spool Often referred to as a file awaiting printing. When outputting data, you may be given the option of spool output, which means output is to file for future processing or printing.

Stand-alone system A computer that is capable of working in isolation from any other system. Most microcomputers are stand-alone systems.

Status A signal indicating whether or not a system is active.

Storage capacity A way of measuring the amount of data that can be stored. Storage capacity is normally measured in Kilobytes (K).

Suite A set of interrelated programs. A term often used instead of package.

Systems analysis The job of analysing systems, both manual and computerised, with the object of implementing new systems or modifying existing ones. The job of a systems analyst will often include implementing systems, a role that requires communications and business management skills as much as computing ones.

Telecommunications Refers to the general concept of sending data from one device to another down a telephone line.

Teleprocessing The use of telecommunications in order to achieve on-line data processing. In other words, to interact with a database from a distance using transmission lines and a terminal.

Telex As part of British Telecom's Datel service, it is used for transmitting text only from one terminal to another, producing printed output at the receiving end.

Test data Data generated and specifically used for testing systems and their software. Often, copies of live data form a useful set of test data. However, test data may have to be created when testing a new system or software program.

Time sharing A technique where a processor shares its time among more than one user. Some operating systems have time-sharing built in to allow costs to be spread by having several users of the system.

Transaction data Any data resulting from a transaction such as a sale, purchase or stock movement. Each such transaction will often be stored as a separate record in a set of transaction files and will be used to update master files.

Turnkey system A system supplied that simply needs switching on and starting. Such systems are normally supplied by outside agencies or consultancy services.

User friendly A term associated with the way some software programs guide a user through processes when using a computer application package.

Utility program A program that can be used to manage files or perform activities outside the normal scope of running a program, e.g. file backup, retrieving lost files and deleting unwanted files.

Validate A process of checking whether data conforms to expected input, such as ensuring alphabetic characters are not entered when the computer expects a number.

Verification A way of confirming that data input is complete and correct or a certain action is what is required (the 'ARE YOU SURE' message).

Visual display unit (VDU) The screen of the computer which displays text and graphic output as soft copy.

Virtual storage This is a technique whereby the computer uses backing store, usually on disk, as part of the processing area in addition to internal memory. This enables the use of very large programs that are normally beyond the memory capabilities of the machine on which they are running. An example is the way in which only a small part of the Sage software is loaded into memory at any one time.

Virus An outside computer program which can disrupt files and is often difficult to detect. Anti-virus programs are available.

Winchester drive A storage device that holds a hard disk. The hard disk is non-removable but offers high storage density and capacity and is generally very reliable.

Window A method of sectioning the VDU in such a way that an operator can see different parts of a document or run different applications at the same time.

Word processing An application that involves processing words and perfecting format, spelling and so on before producing hard copy. Word processors are replacing typewriters at an increasing rate.

Index

Whatever software package you are learning ...

- Aldus PageMaker
- Ami Pro v 2 for Windows
- dBase III
- dBase IV
- dBase IV.1
- DataEase 4
- LocoScript 1 & 2
- LocoScript 1.5
- Lotus 1-2-3
- Microsoft Excell v 3 for Windows
- Microsoft Word for Windows
- Microsoft Word 5.0
- Microsoft Works 2.0
- MS-DOS
- Multiplan
- Pegasus
- Paradox 3.5
- Quattro Pro
- Sage Bookkeeper
- Sage Financial Controller
- Smartware 1
- Supercalc 5
- Symphony 2
- Timeworks Publisher 2
- UNIX
- Ventura Publisher
- WordPerfect 5.0
- WordPerfect 5.1
- Wordstar 4
- Wordstar 1512
- Wordwise

etc

You will find a book in the *Training Guide* series suited to your needs.

Each title follows the same, effective format:

- the text is fully comprehensive yet free of jargon
- instructions are carefully structured
- covers all the main functions of the package
- tasks and activities teach the various commands and reinforce learning

Ask for the titles in the *Training Guide* series in your local bookstore.
Alternatively, contact our marketing department: **Pitman Publishing**,
128 Long Acre, London WC2E 9AN. Telephone 071-379 7383.

OPEN LEARNING SERIES

An increasing number of people are learning word processing skills at home or in the office and sitting their final examinations as an outside student entry. Many college courses are now also based upon open learning techniques. This user-friendly series provides clear and step-by-step instruction to all aspects of each package.

The series provides:

- purpose-build open learning material
- user-friendly and helpful guidance notes
- clear, easy-to-follow instructions
- a logical and consistent layout which offers concise and effective instruction
- self-contained units to allow 'dip-in' learning for those requiring revision within certain areas of application

Titles include:

- Microsoft Word for Windows
- WordPerfect 5.1
- Lotus 1-2-3
- dBase IV.1.1

Ask for the titles in the *Open Learning Series* in your local bookstore. Alternatively, contact our marketing department: **Pitman Publishing**, 128 Long Acre, London WC2E 9AN. Telephone 071-379 7383.